Also published in

Reprints of Economic Classics

by Joseph Dorfman

THE ECONOMIC MIND IN AMERICAN CIVILIZATION I-V [1945-1959]

THORSTEIN VEBLEN AND HIS AMERICA [1934]

Edited by Joseph Dorfman

ESSAYS, REVIEWS AND REPORTS BY THORSTEIN VEBLEN

TYPES OF ECONOMIC THEORY BY WESLEY C. MITCHELL

Reprints of Economic Classics

TWO ESSAYS BY HENRY CARTER ADAMS

TWO ESSAYS

BY

HENRY CARTER ADAMS

RELATION OF THE STATE TO INDUSTRIAL ACTION

&

ECONOMICS AND JURISPRUDENCE

EDITED BY

JOSEPH DORFMAN

WITH AN INTRODUCTORY ESSAY AND NOTES

&

WITH A NEW INTRODUCTION AND APPENDICES

FOR THE 1969 REPRINT

REPRINTS OF ECONOMIC CLASSICS

AUGUSTUS M. KELLEY · PUBLISHERS

NEW YORK 1969

First Edition 1954
Reprinted 1969 by
Augustus M. Kelley • Publishers
New York, N. Y. 10010
By arrangement with Columbia University Press

Library of Congress Catalogue Card Number
75-76510

PRINTED IN THE UNITED STATES OF AMERICA
by SENTRY PRESS, NEW YORK, N. Y. 10019

TWO ESSAYS BY HENRY CARTER ADAMS

Contents

INTRODUCTION TO SECOND EDITION

The publication of a second edition of Henry Carter Adams's two landmark essays in the development of American economic thought and policy has provided the editor with the opportunity to make some additional comments on Adams's work and influence; and to attach two appendices containing a third essay and some illuminating correspondence.

The first edition contained the two essays that gave the volume its title: "The State in Relation to Industrial Action" and "Economics and Jurisprudence." These two essays, as one of the earliest and most perceptive students of Adams has written, represent the core of Adams's contribution to social economics.[1] The additional paper "An Interpretation of the Social Movements of Our Times," which was delivered before the School of Applied Ethics at Plymouth, Massachusetts, in the summer of 1891 and was published in the October 1891 issue of *The International Journal of Ethics* (now *Ethics*), contains not only a summary of the major ideas of the two essays but also the most mature statement of his approach to the dynamic social movements of his time, including the emerging trade union movement.

The three letters in appendix II amplify Adams's position. The first, to President James B. Angell of the University of Michigan, is the one referred to below on p. 32. It was in response to President Angell's request for his views on certain basic socio-economic questions. The president at the time was concerned over Adams's "peculiar notions which seem to verge on

[1]Lazar Volin to Joseph Dorfman, October 7, 1953.

See his "Henry Carter Adams: Critic of Laissez-Faire," *Journal of Social Philosophy*, April 1938. Here on p. 249 he has a long quotation from the third essay to illustrate the point that "Adams was wont to compare modern industrial conflicts to the historic constitutional struggles of the past."

socialism."[2] As the letter reveals he was opposed, as he put it at the time (1886) in the newspaper article, to the "tyranny of German socialism," but also to the "tyranny of Spencerian anarchy." The other two letters, from the papers of Henry Demarest Lloyd (the eminent social reformer) in the State Historical Society of Wisconsin, throw some important side-lights on Adams's then radical idea of labor's proprietary right in industry. Today his views are so much in the mainstream that a president of the United States can extend his notion of proprietary right to assert that every person has "at least one property right—it is the the right to opportunity."[3]

Adams's fame as the pioneer thinker in laying down the underlying economic philosophy of what might be called the modern American welfare state has continued to grow.[4] Thus in 1956 and 1957, for example, the successive presidents of the American Economic Association paid tribute to his penetrating insights. E. E. Witte, at the start of his address in 1956 in "Economics and Public Policy," said "it is noteworthy . . . that the first publication of the American Economic Association was Henry C. Adams's essay on 'The Relation of the State to Industrial Action'—to my way of thinking still one of the soundest treatments of the subject."[5]

The following year 1957, Morris Copeland noted in his address "Institutionalism and Welfare Economics" that "when price competition and competition on other terms of trade are combined, the regulatory function [of the principle of competition] may be impaired. Indeed, in such circumstances, as Henry Carter Adams pointed out long ago, the tendency may be to

[2]Thomas M. Cooley, "Diary," entry of March 30, 1866, in Michigan Historical Collections. The letter is also in the Collections.

[3]Quoted from address of President Johnson before the National Urban League in "Johnson in City, Challenges G.O.P. on Rights Record," *The New York Times*, November 20, 1968.

[4]One of the architects of the New Deal, Isador Lubin, has written the editor: "As you know, I was a great admirer of Adams. He was both a great teacher. and a great philosopher. To top it all, he was a real gentleman." (Lubin to Joseph Dorfman, September 2, 1955.)

[5]*The American Economic Review*, March 1957; Witte, a follower of John R. Commons, was a major architect of the Social Security Act of 1935.

lower the plane of competition and 'force the moral sentiment pervading any trade down to the level of . . . the worst man . . . in it.' "[6]

In more recent years, his work has been a major source of inspiration to the forward looking students in industrial relations, and he has been hailed as the pioneer American thinker in the treatment of trade unionism as part of the democratic process. As the historian of labor union theories in the United States put it, "as a well-informed forerunner of modern trade-union theorists, he was unsurpassed."[7]

Curiously, after the first edition of this book appeared, it seemed that in dominant circles in American economics Adams was viewed as an "offbeat" figure. *The American Economic Review,* the official organ of the American Economic Association, which originally published the first essay in the first volume of the *Publications of the American Economic Association* (1887) and the second, Adams's presidential address before the Association in 1896, in the Association's *Economic Studies* (February 1897), listed the book under the last category "Unclassified."[8]

Today, he still ranks as a major theorist of economic policy.

Columbia University
November 1968

JOSEPH DORFMAN

---

[6]*The American Economic Review,* March 1958, p. 8. Copeland like Witte considered himself a member of the Institutionalist school of economics.

For Adams as one of the great American forerunners of this school, see Joseph Dorfman, "The Background of Institutional Economics," in Dorfman *et al., Institutional Economics—Veblen, Commons and Mitchell Reconsidered* (Berkeley and Los Angeles: University of California Press, 1963) pp. 30-32.

[7]Mark Perlman, *Labor Union Theories in America; Background and Development* (Evanston, Ill.: Row, Peterson, 1958) p. 173. Perlman noted that "Henry Carter Adams may be identified as a link between the American University development of a theory of unionism and the German historical school of economics" (p. 163). On Adams's relation to the German historical school, see Joseph Dorfman, "The Role of the German Historical School in American Economic Thought," *The American Economic Review,* May 1955, pp. 23, 25-27.

[8]*The American Economic Review,* September 1954, p. 733.

INTRODUCTORY ESSAY

Henry Carter Adams: The Harmonizer of Liberty and Reform

BY JOSEPH DORFMAN

THERE ARE ECONOMISTS who sum up in a comprehensive fashion the character of their epoch or who paint in bold strokes the outline of a future order. There are others who function best in the shadows of transition between two merging and yet contrasting epochs. An economist of the latter sort was Henry Carter Adams (1851–1921). He lived when the nineteenth-century tradition of *laissez faire* was first effectively challenged in this country, but when the challengers had not yet visualized clearly the eventual alternatives.

That tradition became solidly rooted in the Jacksonian era. This is not the place for an exposition of the material and intellectual circumstances that made this doctrine harmorious with the development and the needs of a free society. In substance, the Jacksonian era marked the culmination of the attack on the tradition of a feudal, aristocratic society of privilege and perquisites bestowed by law on the few at the expense of the many. It marked the triumph of the idea that, in the absence of law-created privileges, most men could acquire a competence by industry and could become politically independent. The diffusion of property was the safeguard of democratic society. The moral duty of self-assertion became embedded in the principle of competition, for—so it was thought—only the nerveless, parasitic, aristocratic-minded Tory wanted the security of legal monopoly in order to filch an income from the industrious. Closely attuned to and supporting the new tradition was the political economy expounded in the schools, in the press, and from the platform. This was, in general, the English classical political economy, somewhat vulgarized, to be sure, for popular consumption.

But this was the day before the spread of the corporation, the factory, and that most potent instrument of America's first great industrial revolution, the railroad. With their development at a heightened tempo in the post-Civil War era, complicated by the breakdown of monetary standards, there emerged the problem of how to maintain the values of classic liberalism. To sensitive minds the massive strikes, the widespread buccaneering practices of corporations and promoters, the terrifying corruption in politics, seemed almost as characteristic of the seventies and eighties as were the magnificent material developments. There were men who lost their faith in democracy and called for depriving the "rabble," directly or indirectly, of the franchise. Others damned indiscriminately trade unions and large business, though, it must be confessed, more often the former than the latter. Stupendous material interests were opposed to the expansion of state power, but they were not the only sources of opposition, and it is even questionable that they were the most important. Most of the intelligence of the nation was opposed to the use of the power of government beyond its traditional, largely negative role of the protection of the lives of individuals and the contractual rights of property. It was felt generally that the process of reform, once begun, would not end until the country lay under the heel of an absolute dictatorship.

The embattled advocates of *laissez faire* found welcome confirmation in some important developments in the physical as well as the social sciences. Herbert Spencer combined Darwin's epoch-making doctrine of evolution with Sir Henry Maine's famous thesis of the development of society from status to contract to form a comprehensive system of philosophy that began with the first principles of the physical world and ended with an ethics that made uncontrolled competition the end product of the evolutionary process, the means of maintaining "absolute justice." William Graham Sumner, Spencer's American counterpart, was a mighty host in himself. His vast knowledge, busy pen, and powerful presence on the platform were fully utilized to present the ablest and most consistent defense of extreme *laissez faire* this country has ever known.

What Sumner's works lacked in grace and lucidity was supplied by the popular treatises of the Frenchman, Frédéric Bastiat, especially by his *Economic Harmonies.* To be sure, the last great codifier of the English classical political economy, John Stuart Mill, in his widely used *Principles of Political Economy with Some of Their Applications to Social Philosophy,* had contended that expediency and not the doctrine of *laissez faire* should govern the role of the state in industrial affairs, in any specific case. But expediency was hardly a principle, and the result was a miscellaneous series of individual instances reluctantly admitted as temporary exceptions to the principle of *laissez faire.*

Against the "tyranny of Spencerian anarchy," there arose a variety of protests. The few socialists of the Marxian variety were a motley crowd, in whom Marx himself would hardly have recognized his disciples. Far more potent was Henry George's spectacular doctrine. *Progress and Poverty* caught the discontent of the hour and stirred up a tremendous interest in economics. Yet his panacea of the "single-tax," while it found much acceptance for dealing with problems concerning natural resources—especially forests, mines, and city lands—seemed at best a roundabout solution of those of labor and monopoly. Here and there a thinker of established reputation, like General Francis A. Walker, cautiously questioned extreme *laissez faire.* He aroused the ire of his learned colleagues but furnished inspiration to younger men.

The most constructive opposition eventually came from a group of economists who grew to maturity in the long depression following the Panic of 1873. They had a desire to achieve social reform with the aid of a humanized and more adequate economic theory than had been their college diet. They were not from the ranks of the proletariat. They came from families of considerable culture and sometimes wealth. They were moved by the ideals of the Christian Socialists of the middle of the century, who were led by the saintly Frederick Denison Maurice of King's College, London, and they placed their faith in voluntary producers' cooperatives. Such "economic republicanism" would bulwark political democracy. But until the ideal was achieved, the state as well as the church and other voluntary associations must play a positive role in industry to protect the community. This must be done without stifling enterprise whose spur was the hope of profit, for upon this, great material advances rested.

These men generally did their graduate work in Germany, universally acknowledged as the outstanding center of scholarship in practically all fields and certainly in that of the infant social sciences. The Germany of Bismarck seemed to them an example of both efficiency and enlightened social reform and a warning against the danger to liberty implicit in too generous state intervention. Their authentic counterparts were found in England rather than in Germany. Men like Arnold Toynbee were spiritually close to them. It was Toynbee who said in *Lectures on the*

Industrial Revolution of the Eighteenth Century in England,

Competition is neither good nor evil in itself; it is a force which has to be studied and controlled; it may be compared to a stream whose strength and direction have to be observed, that embankments may be thrown up within which it may do its work harmlessly and beneficially.

As the two essays reprinted here amply prove, Henry Carter Adams was a powerful voice in this stirring, questioning group. Hence, it may seem surprising that these essays have been all but forgotten. The quasi-Hegelian idiom in which they are written certainly limited their fame, but more important was the fact that until 1929, the problems of competition, state intervention, rights of capital and labor, seemed less urgent than they had been to Adams's contemporaries.

Today, we are struck by these essays' appropriateness to the current scene. They were forged in the heat of social turmoil and intellectual upheavals not unlike our own. Naturally, their concrete suggestions may no longer be relevant, but they are the kind of scarce "old stuff" which suggests new insights as long as we remain committed, in Adams's own language, to the "realization [as a conscious ideal] of a conservative, self-respecting, self-controlled democracy."[1]

Adams's story is the story of a practitioner of an infant social science in an age astir with intellectual as well as material progress. His task was to redeem economics from the contempt of the business community and the suspicions of workingmen. In its performance, he was forced to face the problems of political and social democracy. Having decided, after a struggle with himself, on an academic career,

[1]Adams, "The Graduate School," *Inlander,* 3:314 (April, 1893).

he found it no easy matter to gain even a precarious foothold from which he could begin his work. And once having done so, he faced the problems that have continued to plague the land: monopoly and the "social question," monetary disorders, and business depressions. In an age when businessmen often spoke as if they had a first mortgage on civilization and the "anarchists of the deed" proclaimed the merits of bombs, it required courage and patience to plead for orderly reform. To devise procedures sufficiently flexible to meet the new developments yet immune to the disorder of bureaucratic routine was paramount. The task was complicated by the lack of adequate, even approximately accurate, factual data. Social inventiveness of a high order was called for, if liberty was to be maintained. That quality Adams exhibited in his use of statistics and accounting as instruments of public control, and in his appeal to the Anglo-American tradition of common and statute law. It was as a conserver of the spirit of liberty embodied in that tradition that he pleaded for reform. And his success, though quite modest by modern standards, was brilliant testimony to the vitality of the tradition of peaceful adjustment through the democratic process, that is, "conservative," in the best sense of that abused term.

Of his faith in democracy, there could be no question. Only a rooted democrat could have declared,

> It has become quite fashionable to smile at the Declaration of Independence, because it contains some phrasing that has not stood the test of careful analysis. But such a smile indicates intellectual weakness rather than strength since it shows that one cares more for words than for the spirit of an age or the truth of an idea so great that it moved a generation.[2]

[2]Adams, "On the Education of Statesmen," *Princeton Review*, 58:33 (January, 1884).

Henry Carter Adams was born in 1851 in Davenport, Iowa, and was reared in that then frontier state.[3] He came from an old New England family, whose forbears had migrated from Shropshire, England, in 1628. His father, Ephraim, had joined some fellow graduates of Andover Theological Seminary in 1843 to form the famous Iowa Band. They dedicated their lives to erecting a Christian commonwealth west of the Mississippi. Ephraim Adams helped to start sturdy Iowa College (now Grinnell College) in 1846, as a part of his missionary task.

Largely because of ill health, young Adams had had only one year of formal education before entering Iowa College at the age of nineteen. The college gave a rather thorough training in spite of its limited resources. The president, the Reverend George F. Magoun, as was customary, taught seniors the social sciences as part of his field of "Mental, Moral, Political, and Christian Science." These social sciences included "Political Science," "Political Economy," and "The Constitution of the United States."

Adams was a good student, especially in "literature and metaphysical subjects," and he did exceptionally well in political economy.[4] By his junior year, in 1873, Adams had formed the idea of starting a school of political science for

[3]For a general biographical account of Adams, see S. Lawrence Bigelow, I. Leo Sharfman, and R. M. Wenley, "Henry Carter Adams," *Journal of Political Economy*, 30:201–11 (April, 1922); see also Marvin B. Rosenberry, "Henry Carter Adams," in *Michigan and the Cleveland Era*, ed. Earl D. Babst and Lewis G. Vander Velde (Ann Arbor, 1948), pp. 24–41.

A number of Adams's letters to Professor E. R. A. Seligman which are in the Seligman papers of the Seligman Library of Economics at the Columbia University Library have been published in "The Seligman Correspondence," II, ed. Joseph Dorfman, *Political Science Quarterly* 56:270–79 (June, 1941).

[4]Magoun to Daniel C. Gilman, June 9, 1876, Johns Hopkins University Alumni Office.

the training of future statesmen, but his father wanted him to become a minister. Upon graduation from college he spent a year teaching in the lower schools of Iowa, and then proceeded, with some reluctance, to Andover Theological Seminary. Before the year was over Adams decided to become a "first class writer in civic themes." He was ambitious to launch a new political journal. He prepared an elaborate philosophical prospectus which he sent to leading editors and college presidents for comment. The press of the country, and especially the periodicals, were the only political educator, he wrote, but they suffered from lack of devotion to "purely political and historical aims." His organ would present significant events in a clear, concise "logical order so that every man, by following the natural workings of his own mind, can deduce their principles." Great emphasis would be placed on literature, for a country's literature "more unmistakably than anything else indicates the character of the national mind." Edwin L. Godkin, whose *Nation*, Adams rightly felt, was the best American journal, expressed sympathy for the youth's ambition, but told him the magazine would need "an enormous fund of resources."

Fortunately for Adams, Johns Hopkins University opened in 1876 as the first substantial graduate school in the country and offered ten fellowships of $500 each. In applying, Adams forthrightly stated that he felt that training in political science and political economy, rather than working one's self up from reporter, promised to be the road to an editor's chair in the future. On the other hand, J. Henry Thayer, of Andover Theological Seminary, in endorsing this application, expressed the hope that Adams might "prevail upon himself to abandon all thought of 'short cuts' and premature aspirations after an editor's chair."[5] Adams received a fellowship and showed such promise that it was renewed the following year. Johns Hopkins was better equipped in the older established fields of mathematical and physical sciences than in the social sciences. In this area the teaching was in the hands of nonresident lecturers, and Adams and other fellows helped out.

After receiving in 1878 the first doctorate in the social sciences, or, as it is called at Johns Hopkins, in Political Science, Adams went abroad for a year of further training, at President Daniel C. Gilman's suggestion and by means of a loan from Francis White, a trustee of the university. After brief stays at Oxford and Heidelberg, he proceeded to Berlin to study with Adolf Wagner, a leader of the moderate wing of the German Historical School, and of the movement for moderate social reform with the help of the church and the state. Through Wagner, Adams was invited to participate in the celebrated seminar in statistics conducted by Ernst Engel, head of the Prussian Statistical Bureau, the foremost statistician of Europe and author of the famous "law" of consumption. Adams then went to the University of Paris to investigate the relationship between economic doctrine and democratic ideas in France. He proceeded to Bonn, where Adolf Held, one of the ablest of the younger members of the historical school, was busy on his *Zwei Bücher zur sozialen Geschichte Englands* (posthumously published in 1880), a work that proved to be one of the most profound as well as a pioneering book on the Industrial Revolution in England and its relation to the classical political economy. Held convinced Adams that the

[5]The manuscript of the prospectus for the journal and the correspondence on the application for the fellowship are in the Alumni Office of Johns Hopkins University.

latter's interest in the development of political economy called primarily for the examination of original sources in England, and so Adams found himself at the British Museum in the summer of 1879.[6]

As the period for his studies in Europe was ending, Adams concerned himself with the prospects for an academic career. What did he have to "sell"? He had grown up in an atmosphere of rampant economic individualism. His own testimony is that at the outset of his studies, in his college years, he adhered to the "extreme school." But at Johns Hopkins he came under the influence of a somewhat modified type of economic liberal, General Francis A. Walker, the best-known American economist.

As director of the 1870 Census, Walker had come to appreciate the complexities of the American economy. He held that the English classical school, devoid of crude apologetics as presented by its last eminent exponent, John Elliot Cairnes, furnished the basic skeleton of political economy, but that the flesh and blood must be supplied from something along the lines of what was being developed in Europe by the historical school—what he understood to mean historico-statistical work. Walker was among the first to question successfully the famous wages-fund doctrine, which reduced the determination of wages to the simple arithmetic of dividing the amount of capital by the number of laborers seeking work. He favored moderate state intervention in the areas of factory sanitation and protection of women and children. He also supported the restoration of the bimetallic standard by international agreement on the ground that the gold standard provided an inade-

[6]Adams to Andrew D. White, July 31, 1879, White Papers, Cornell University Library.

quate supply of money for expanding business and resulted in long-enduring (secular) stagnation and severe depression.

It is probable that Walker shook Adams's complacency. Adams became interested in social reform, including the cooperative movement. This interest became more systematic during his sojourn in Europe, particularly in Germany. He wrote Gilman, on December 15, 1878, that the subject currently claiming his attention was the "much talked of 'humbug' Socialism." He said he put humbug in quotation marks, not because he was a socialist or had any faith in the socialist plan, but because he did not "fully agree with those who thoughtlessly use the word." According to Adams, though socialism could not be realized, it had great influence in molding the economic thought of his day.

> [Some of its criticisms of] the English system of industry are just, and true. . . . The characteristic criticism, respecting the injurious workings of free competition is . . . most significant as pointing out the great economic problem of the present. . . . The recognition of this has given me again my old feeling of enthusiasm over the future of political economy as a study, and its power to benefit mankind. The first period of enthusiasm was based on entire ignorance of the factors to be studied, and since coming from that period I have studied economy rather as a stepping stone to a political philosophy, but it turns out that Economy in the extended meaning of that word, is that philosophy, and I am willing to drop the high sounding phrase for the reality.[7]

[7]Adams to Gilman, December 15, 1878, Johns Hopkins University Library.

Adams sought to popularize the term "economy," and later "economics," to cover the discipline usually called "political economy." The latter he restricted to "private finance" or the domain of "industrial" or "voluntary" association. As coordinate with "Political Economy," he proposed "The Science of Finance" or "Public Finance" to cover the domain of "coercive organization"—"the wants of the State and the means by which those wants may be supplied." Thus, "Political Economy" and "The Science of Finance" were the two branches of "Economy." Adams, *The Science of Finance* (New

He was aware, of course, that even mild social reform was too strong for the academic atmosphere. He felt, therefore, that he ought to develop a competence in a more technical field. The field of public finance was prominent in Germany, but practically nonexistent in Anglo-American universities. He suggested to Gilman a comprehensive two-year program of four courses. First, there would be a course—an unusual one—the "Principles of Political Economy," stressing the progress of economic doctrine in its relation to civilization and introducing historical accounts of attempts and plans to better economic conditions. Then there should be a course on public finance, including financial machinery and administration, principles of public loans and taxation, and administration of public lands and enterprises, such as ports, the marine, the army, and the customs. In this area he proposed, in addition, a more specialized course on the "Financial History of the United States," which would include tariffs, money, and banking.

Novel to academic ears was his proposal for a course on "American Technics," which would comprise the contributions of agriculture, manufacturing, and transportation. The lectures, he said, should be supplemented by abundant illustrations from statistics. As part of his general program, Adams also urged Gilman to set up a school of "statecraft" or political science.[8]

York, 1898), pp. 1–2; Adams, "The Relation of the Science of Finance to Allied Sciences," in *Congress of Arts and Science, Universal Exposition, St. Louis, 1904,* ed. Howard J. Rogers (Boston and New York), 7:182.

[8]Most of the American students in Germany were interested in that area, Adams said, and he added that if a good School of History, Economy, and Philosophy were established, sufficient students would be attracted. (Adams to Gilman, August 4, 1878. Johns Hopkins University Library.) Adams was heralding a movement that in 1880 was realized when John W. Burgess and others established at Columbia a School of Political Science.

Gilman, however, seems to have felt that circumstances did not warrant more than a two-month course on political economy, and that this could be handled along with history by the newly appointed associate, Herbert Baxter Adams, a former fellow and a promising historian. Fortunately for our Adams, the confusion of names led to an opening at Cornell. The usual limited instruction in political economy was already provided for at Cornell through the Professor of Moral and Intellectual Philosophy. But President Andrew D. White, then Ambassador to Germany, needed a substitute for his own courses in history and interviewed Henry Carter Adams, believing that he was Herbert Baxter. However, White was impressed with Adams's syllabus of proposed lectures on political economy. On Adams's return to the United States in the fall of 1879, he was appointed by the acting president, William C. Russel, to give a series of twenty-five lectures on "Money, Banking and Finance" to the seniors during the January-March quarter of 1880. Gilman then arranged that Adams be appointed as assistant at Johns Hopkins and follow his Cornell engagement with a two-month course on "Money and Banking" and a series of nine public lectures on "National Debts."

The next semester Adams realized his wish to give the course on the principles of "Political Economy" at Johns Hopkins. In his report on the term's work, he emphasized that "if it is to become practical, political economy must cease to be studied as the philosophy of enlightened self-interest and be made a branch of general jurisprudence."[9] Adams at this time was also increasing his knowledge of "American technics" through his work with the Census of 1880 of which Walker was again the director.

[9]Adams to Gilman, December 18, 1880, Johns Hopkins University Alumni Office.

In the second semester the University of Michigan provided Adams with an opportunity to better his academic position. With President James Burrell Angell on leave as Minister to China, Adams was appointed lecturer to cover Angell's two two-hour courses. The Michigan authorities were impressed with Adams, and he stayed on for the first semester each year. The salary of $800 ($1,100 beginning in 1882) for the term—the same as at Johns Hopkins—was hardly enough, but fortunately after the lapse of a year he was able to revive his connection with Cornell.

This had not been easy. He had by usual standards been successful in his first series of Cornell lectures. Russel, the acting president, wrote to White that Adams was "very modest, simple and unpretending. The boys like the lectures and like him." White was especially impressed by the enthusiasm of one of the students, George L. Burr, who was his own private secretary (and who became a distinguished mediaeval historian). However, when White began urging Russel to reengage Adams with a view to an eventual permanent arrangement, Russel found insuperable objections. He thought Adams "too young." Adams, he said, lacked the "realism that comes from conversation with . . . any one of a hundred New York bankers." Thus, in criticizing the excessive use of loans by governments as against taxes, Adams said in class, according to Russel, that "conservatism being bound to material interests is always an obstruction to progress." And, Russel added, from twelve lectures by a man of reputation like Sumner students would learn more than from a term with an inexperienced man like Adams.[10]

[10]Russel to White, February 1, March 7, 1880, White Papers, Cornell University Library. Burr to White, January 16, 1880, Burr Papers, Cornell University Library.

Russel suggested that every other year Adams might be appointed to give a series of lectures. However, when White returned to Cornell, he obtained the appointment of Adams as a Nonresident Professor of Political Economy to give instruction in the spring quarter of 1882 at a salary of $800 for the two months. The following year Adams was appointed on a two-year basis as Associate Professor of Political Economy, with a half quarter of additional teaching and a raise in salary to $1,375.

From the start Adams viewed political economy, including commercial education, not only as an "analytic science," but also as a constructive study seeking to provide a rational basis for the formation and government of industrial society. The phrase "industrial society" he emphasized was not, as some thought, vague, but stood for a fact of everyday experience.

It has life and movement and, therefore, a history; it has parts and functions and, therefore, organization; it has form and purpose and, therefore, institutions; it has rights and duties and, therefore, a scheme of law; it is fitted into the political system, and for that reason presents a theory of government; it rests upon trust and responsibility, and on that account involves a theory of morals.[11]

Adams's early publications, including the two editions of his *Outline of Lectures upon Political Economy* (1881 and 1886), revealed a reformist bent. The *Outline* was the first American textbook to present W. Stanley Jevons's "new theory of value"—the theory of marginal utility, as it came more popularly to be called. Adams pointed out that this theory assumed in the traditional fashion that "man is a rational animal capable of calculating the future." It re-

[11]Adams, "Relation of the University to Business," *Michigan Alumnus*, 7:92 (December, 1900).

garded "economic quantities as made up of successive increments." This in turn leads to the "law of varying utility." As the "quantity of any commodity decreases, the intensity of the utility of any part of that which remains increases, until at last the commodity becomes indispensable, that is, the utility becomes infinite."

From this he obtained a formula for determining value. By comparing the visible supply of a given commodity with "the pretty well-defined demand" for it at a given time, "we shall discover the final degree of utility which it bears, viz., the utility of the last increment which is always the portion about to be sold." Similarly, the "utility of all commodities is unconsciously estimated and . . . a basis is secured for determining the ratio of exchange between them," that is, value. The law of value then is that "commodities placed upon a market for sale will tend to exchange in a ratio inversely to their degrees of final utility."

The change of view as to the best measure of value, from the labor of the producer as in the older classical political economy to utility to the consumer, was not occasioned, Adams later declared, by the need of a defense against socialism, but developed as a "logical necessity in order to interpret the law of supply and demand and to come to clear understanding of the laws of market price."[12] At the same time he pointed out the contributions of the older classical school, including the Malthusian doctrine of population and its allied doctrine of rent. The most fundamental law, the one that controlled the productivity of land brought under cultivation, he said, was the "law of diminishing returns.

[12]Adams, *Outline of Lectures upon Political Economy*, 1881 ed. (Baltimore), pp. 35–36; 1886 ed. (Ann Arbor, Mich.), pp. 23–24. Adams, "Ten Years of Political Economy in the United States," *Inlander*, 1:23 (March, 1891).

. . . Every increase of production from land is obtained by means of more than a proportional increase in the application of labor and capital to land." Since the price of agricultural produce must cover the cost of that portion of the necessary supply raised under the most unfavorable circumstances, rent was the "surplus of profit on capital invested upon the land."

Such "surplus profit" would come to the cultivating farmer largely to the extent that he was landlord, that is, where land ownership was widely diffused. Thus on the vital issue of Irish land reform, Adams followed John Stuart Mill in support of "peasant proprietorships." It would increase productivity, largely through permanent improvements, because "the mainspring of all activity"—self-interest—was embodied in the magic of property. The hope for its realization, he declared, lay with the British Liberal party, which, under Gladstone, had already taken the first steps to protect the tenant. Adams pointed with approval to the proposal of one of its leaders, the noted Quaker and champion of removal of tariff barriers, John Bright, that the government acquire land by purchase of all estates offered on the market and the "forced sale" of all lands held by all corporations of various sorts, and then dispose of these lands in small farms on thirty-six year's time. "This is liberalism, the recognition of the claims of the lower classes."[13]

On wages, Adams criticized the wages-fund doctrine and presented a less rigid view. He declared in 1884 that

> the rate of wages in a country depends upon . . . the quality of the soil and freedom of access to it, the grade of labor as affecting

[13]Adams, *Outline of Lectures* (1886 ed.), pp. 10, 40. Adams, "The Irish Land Question," *New Englander*, 40:83–84 (January, 1881).

its productivity, and . . . the extent to which the laborers are wisely organized.[14]

In this lay implicit his later position, expressed in a letter:

I fail to find satisfaction in reasoning upon wages which does not rest upon the opinion that the matter is very largely one of diplomacy and controversy between organized interests. The theoretic question . . . proceeds no farther than to lay down certain very loosely defined limits beyond which the contending parties cannot go in their encroachment upon the dividends demanded by the others.[15]

Expressing doubts that the existing system was truly competitive, Adams stressed the claims of the "modified" historical method. "The historical school," had organized the successful revolt against the extreme so-called "scientific" method of English writers, which yielded some conclusions out of harmony with observed facts. The founders properly pointed out that the best way would be to inquire first after realities, rather than to proceed from assumed and unproved premises, and that this could best be done by observing the development of industrial life. The followers of the more adequate modified historical school such as Wagner and Held, argue that the use of "good logic and a priori reasoning" were as necessary as ever.[16]

This was Adams's position, too. He was critical of the methods of the dominant school of classical political econ-

[14]Adams, "Free Trade vs. Protection," II, Rochester (New York) *Daily Union and Advertiser*, March 26, 1884.

[15]Adams to J. B. Clark, J. B. Clark Papers, in possession of J. M. Clark. The page containing the date is missing, but the letter was probably written around 1901. The discussion was continued in a letter from Clark to Adams, dated August 12, 1901. Adams Papers, in possession of the Adams family, Ann Arbor, Michigan.

[16]Adams, "Roscher's National Economy," *Nation*, February 2, 1882. For Adams's authorship, see *The Nation's Index of Titles and Contributors*, Vol. 1, compiled by Daniel C. Haskell (New York, 1953).

omy. He protested against the free and unguarded use of analogy with the physical sciences.

> Development of a physical science consists in the discovery of truths which are assumed always to have existed. . . . Development of a social science, on the other hand, consists partly in the new discovery of old truths, and partly *in observing new truths to emerge from the growth of the social organism.*

He also protested against what he called the "astronomical method" of investigation in the social sciences. He described this method as building a system of thought on the assumption that a certain line is straight, and then taking a "squint to see how crooked it is."

No more effective answer has yet been given to the continued Spencerian cry that *laissez faire* was merely the application to industrial affairs of the "law" that the fittest should survive than Adams's retort that, within bounds, society was capable of directing its own development, for the "fittest type to survive may first exist in the conscious purpose of society, and be realized by means of an environment arbitrarily determined." The " 'lego-historic' facts, although they may vary from time to time," he pointed out, were just as important as the permanent facts of nature.

> As the stroke of the shuttle is limited by the framework of the loom, so the industrial movements of men are bound by the liberties of law and of custom; and, to carry the metaphor a step further, the industrial weaving of society is largely determined by its legal structure. . . . Every change in law means a modification in rights; and when familiar rights are changed, or, what amounts to the same thing, when new duties are imposed, the plane of action for all members of society is adjusted to a new idea.[17]

[17]Adams, "Economics and Jurisprudence" and "Another View of Economic Laws and Methods," *Science*, 1886; reprinted in *Science Economics Discussion*, ed. R. T. Ely (New York, 1886), pp. 81–82, 86, 101–103.

The attention Adams gave to what has since been called "business cycles" was also not usual for a professed theorist. These constantly recurring periods of commercial depression, he held, were an evil which impeded more than any other the rapid development of industrial well being and national improvement. But as yet there was no completely satisfactory explanation of these "commercial fluctuations." The most common theory centered on crises or panics and found their cause in some disturbance of the circulating medium or in abuse of credit.[18] Under this theory panics can be quickly ended if banks follow the well-known rule of Walter Bagehot that they should discount freely at high rates in times of strain, but, in addition, that the government should do all in its power to furnish an adequate supply of "paying medium." This Adams elaborated to mean that the government should stand ready to take government bonds in exchange for legal-tender paper money, convertible, however, into specie.[19]

He presented with some sympathy the theory which directed study primarily to depression, and held that the solution was in a more equitable distribution of income. It called attention to the fact that sales at profitable rates were impossible unless those for whose wants the goods

[18]"The adequate cause, so far as it is purely American, of the late depression [1873–78], is found in the contraction of values which must inevitably follow every period of widespread inflation." Adams, "Payment of Public Debts," *International Review*, 11:256, September, 1881. He held the familiar notion of an "industrial cycle" as comprising ten years. Adams, "Michigan Railroad Appraisal: The Valuation of the Non-Physical Element in Railways," in *Publications of the Michigan Political Science Association* (Ann Arbor, Mich.), 4:74 (June, 1901).

[19]This "interference" by government was criticized by the foremost student of money and banking in the country, on the general ground that it was practically impossible for a government official to decide whether a panic was healthful or not. Horace White, "Adams' *Public Debts*," II, *Nation*, 45:219 (September 15, 1887). For White's authorship, see *Poole's Index to Periodical Literature, 1887–92*, 3:113.

were produced had adequate purchasing power. He noted that the theory applied to a "progressive society" for upon a guaranty of stable demand, production could adjust itself to any rate of distribution.[20]

Such were Adams's views on the broader issues of economics. His application of them filtered through his old background of *laissez faire,* and his more recent interest in reform led to a defense of free trade in the international realm, of limited bimetallism, of moderate state intervention, and of collective bargaining in the labor field.

On foreign trade, he opposed a protective tariff on the basis of the traditional doctrine of classical economics of "comparative advantage," formulated by Mill. Said Adams:

Two people may trade together when the one has the advantage [of facilities of production] in producing everything, but each will export that for which it has the greatest comparative advantage and each will reap benefit from the exchange. It does not therefore follow that when Congress sees that something can be done or produced in the country, it should pass a law to compel people to buy of the home producer.[21]

[20]In developing this theory, Adams was one of the few economists to see merit in Frederick B. Hawley's doctrine that "consumption is necessary to the rapid conversion of 'dead stock' into 'active stock.' " See also what appears to be Adams's work, the review of Hawley's *Population and Capital* in the *Nation,* 35:17–18 (July 6, 1882).

One of Adams's later formulations of the general overproduction or underconsumption theory appeared in his Commencement Address at Rockford College in 1892 ("The Ministry of Wealth," *Rockford Collegian,* November, 1892): "Unless the opulence which comes with the gratuitous service of nature results in the lightening of toil and in raising the standard of living, for the mass of mankind, the ability to produce wealth, which comes with machinery, will be destroyed because the inducement to produce wealth will be paralyzed."

[21]Adams, "Free Trade vs. Protection," I, Rochester (New York) *Daily Union and Advertiser,* March 19, 1884. Adams's first publication was on the tariff issue: Adams, "Zur Geschichte der Besteuerung in den Vereinigten Staaten von Amerika in der Periode von 1789–1816," *Zeitschrift für die gesammte Staatswissenschaft,* 35:719–54 (1879).

The ideal was a tariff for revenue only, but Adams proposed to reach it gradually. The first step was extending the free list to include all raw materials.

His bimetallism led to controversy with Sumner and an exposition of the nature of economic law. A limited amount of bimetallism had been introduced by the Bland-Allison Act of 1878, which provided for government purchase of from two to four million dollars of silver monthly to be coined into silver dollars at the old ratio of 16 to 1. This had by no means stopped the agitation. In 1883, in the midst of another depression, as the federal government continued to repay rapidly the national debt, as Adams had advocated, the complaint was made that this reduced the effective money supply, since the issue of national bank notes was based on federal bonds. To alleviate the contraction, Adams, in the influential business organ *Bradstreet's*, supported the suggestion advanced by J. W. Sylvester, of the United States Assay Office, that legal-tender bullion silver certificates be issued and be redeemable in gold at the market value of silver. Adams declared that "public sentiment is a fact of which legislation must take account and in the presence of strongly marked conflicting sentiments, it frequently occurs that judicious compromise was all that either party can hope or expect." Those who hold that the laws of political economy are independent of a nation's sentiments, as expressed in its legislative enactments, would be guilty of the error of "reasoning from premises without an appeal to facts." Sumner promptly replied on behalf of the "scientific economists." He accused Adams of confusing politics and economics in paying attention to expedient measures, for tradition and fashion "had nothing to do with the laws of money as deduced by science," as a matter of nature's forces.

Adams retorted by broadening the issue.

> My position on monetary laws is that habit, character, prejudice, degree of education, state of social development and the like (these may or may not be expressed in legislative enactments) are essential for determining the monetary conduct of people.

Since every law of political economy was a law of human conduct, human sentiment was its characteristic element. There were no "nature's forces," as Sumner claimed, in monetary science. There was a basic difference between the inclination of potatoes to sprout, the inclination to believe two and two are four, and the inclination which compels men to conduct their business according to certain rules. A science might be based upon any of these sets of facts but they were sciences of a different character. To insist that the study of political economy proceed according to the methods of mathematics and physics was to proceed irrespective of the facts.

Sumner holds that Gresham's law was a "nature's force," but, according to Adams, on analysis it was simply a convenient way of stating that men have an inclination to keep the good money and give their neighbors bad when either serves equally well for a single exchange. Again, take the scientific character of the law that prices fluctuate with the amount of circulation. "This, too, is only an easy way of saying that every man insists that his money shall get into circulation because, as we now use money, he can thereby get a profit. . . . Call up Abraham and see if the price of his flocks and slaves varied with 'the amount of circulation.' " The business tendency which it disclosed, was true "only of people with a certain history at their back." To call it a natural force was "mental provincialism."

Since John Stuart Mill's time, Adams bluntly stated, there was not a

single economic problem solved, or a single step taken toward a better understanding of the economic questions of the present by any member of the school of writers to which Professor Sumner has attached himself. But, they ask, is not our method logical? Yes, the method is logical. What, then, do you complain of? I complain that it is totally inadequate to the demands now made upon the student of industrial science.

It was at this time that Adams expressed the opinion that the country badly needed at the helm a man like Thomas Jefferson's hardheaded, enlightened Secretary of the Treasury, Albert Gallatin.

[He was] a strong and a conservative Democrat, the type of man that we want now, that indeed we must have if the trend of our future state is to be such as we may approve. Gallatin hated aristocracy, were he alive now he would hate the money power with a righteous hatred and that is what must give the aggressive power & conviction to the next movements in history, in Europe as well as in this Country.[22]

The questions uppermost in Adams's mind concerned the role of the state and law in industrial affairs. He had long advocated that the state should have an expanded role. Taking his cue from Wagner, he declared before the American Association for Social Science that history showed that as countries grew more populous and the social and industrial relations more complex, the functions of government must

[22]H. C. Adams to Herbert Baxter Adams, April 22, 1883, Johns Hopkins University Library.

Adams at the time deprecated the indecisiveness of the Democratic party. Adams to David A. Wells, March 28, 1884, in Wells Papers, New York Public Library.

extend to continually new fields. He especially noted the need for forest conservation, because of the frequent recurrence of floods, the more rapid increase and marked alternation of drought and wet, the progress of farming toward the exhaustion of lands, and so forth. Corporations would not do the work, for the time was too remote for the fruits of the investment. Such matters should be left to the states and municipalities for the expansion of the national authority as well as of private corporations represented to him a "tendency toward centralization . . . too rapid to be . . . healthy."[23]

These principles, however, hardly furnished guides in handling the overpowering questions of factory legislation, monopoly, and, above all, relations between employees and employers, projected by the upheavals of the seventies. The agitation against "monopoly" was greatly heightened by the fear that the trend threatened to engulf all industry. The already weak railroad regulation was rendered even less effective by the Supreme Court decision of 1886 in *Wabash, St. Louis and Pacific Railroad Company v. Illinois*, which denied the right of state commissions to fix rates if interstate commerce was involved. A movement was launched for an interstate commerce commission. At the same time the nation was witnessing a series of strikes. In 1885 came a successful strike by the Knights of Labor against Jay Gould's Southwestern Railroad System. In February of the following year the Knights attempted to repeat the performance, but the tactics of the leadership and the violence that ensued

[23]Adams, "On State Repudiation." Abstract of an address before the (Johns Hopkins) Historical and Political Science Association, December, 1880, in *Johns Hopkins University Circulars*, January, 1881, p. 96. Adams, "The Financial Standing of the States," *Journal of Social Science*, No. 19 (1885), p. 46.

brought dismal failure. Meanwhile under the sanction of the American Federation of Labor strikes to gain the eight-hour day were going on at an intensified pace. In connection with this movement, the Haymarket bombing episode of May 4, 1886, occurred in Chicago and unleashed considerable hysteria in the country. Little distinction was drawn between the "anarchists of the deed," to whom the bombing was attributed, and other kinds of socialist and even liberal movements. Henry George's vigorous mayoralty campaign in New York City intensified the hysteria as his opponents denounced him as a robber, nihilist, communist, and bloody anarchist.

In March, 1886, before the Constitution Club of New York and again before the Institute of Social Science, composed of reform-minded, well-to-do citizens, Adams delivered a paper on "Principles that Should Control the Interference of the States in Industries." This, in elaborated form, became the famous monograph called "Relation of the State to Industrial Action," which is reprinted in this volume. It insisted that "public regulation must proceed *pari passu* with the development of private trade. The true idea of society is not *laissez faire*, but economic freedom and freedom is the child, not the enemy of law and regulation."[24]

Laissez faire, declared Adams, was the dominant habit of thought and action, but its authority rested simply upon its *de facto* existence, that is, "the instinct of conservatism" which, by historical accident, operated against the expanding functions of government. In Germany where the State rather than the individual was dominant in industrial

[24]T. S. Adams and Helen Sumner, *Labor Problems* (New York, 1905), p. 25.

society, the conservative tradition was opposed to individual initiative. The American view must emphasize the complementary relations of the State and the individual in the development of the social organism.

There were two important functions that government could perform in the industrial area. First, the state could determine the plane of competition. Free competition tended to lower the moral sense of the community, to force businessmen to the moral level of the most unscrupulous competitor. Those fitted to survive unregulated competition would be the very ones who were morally the least fit to survive. Thus legislation did not curtail competition but simply raised its plane. It removed serious abuses without eliminating the benefit of individual action. Adams's example was significant, because it illustrated the scope of the doctrine. Suppose the absence of factory acts and ten manufacturers competing for the supply of a market. Nine of them, if in control of affairs, might not want to "weave into their fabrics the lives of helpless children." But since the moral sense of the tenth was indifferent, the great majority must adhere to his merciless level or be thrown out of the market. In such cases the state must step in and say to the few, "You must do business as the better elements of society wish it to be done."[25]

The state may also realize for society the benefit of monopoly. For this purpose Adams developed the far-reaching principle of "increasing returns." He divided industries into three classes. (1) Industries of "constant returns" were

[25]The quotations in the last paragraph are from Adams's review of W. Stanley Jevons, *The State in Relation to Labour*, in the *Nation*, 35:271 (September 28, 1882). The authorship of this review is missing in Haskell's *The Nation's Index*, but the same illustration was used in the monograph, and also in "An Interpretation of the Social Movements of Our Time," *International Journal of Ethics*, October, 1891.

those where an increase of capital and labor yielded a proportionate increase of product. (2) Industries with "diminishing returns" comprised those where the increase was not proportionate. (3) Industries of "increasing returns" were those where the result was a progressive increase of product. The first and second categories included the great mass of businesses and agriculture, and called for no government interference. Individual interest here gave the most efficient results. But industries of the third category, which usually take the corporate form, must be subject to control as "natural monopolies" for here free competition is incapable of protecting the public.[26] Using the railroad as an example of increasing returns, Adams declared that in such industries free competition was powerless to exercise a healthy regulative influence. It was easier for an established business to extend its facilities to meet a new demand than for a new industry to spring into competitive existence. According to the law of "increasing returns," every measure by which an increase of tonnage could be secured was entirely defensible. Any competition in industries of increasing returns was of piratical, cutthroat, short-term nature, ending in monopoly, with the community paying the cost of

[26]Adams agreed that the classification of diminishing, constant, and increasing returns was that of John Stuart Mill, except in so far as the law of increasing returns was substituted for Mill's consideration of monopoly prices. But he rightly felt that the phenomena of increasing returns had been little discussed previously.

Adams later explicitly recognized that the "law of increasing returns" might require modification if and when the limits of full capacity and economies of scale were reached in the affected industries, but the existence of such a condition could only be determined by investigation. Adams, testimony, April 7, 1900, *Testimony Taken By The Commission to Investigate The Postal Service*, 56th Congress, 2d session, *Senate Documents*, No. 89, part 2 (Washington, 1901), pp. 444–45.

As Dr. Lazar Volin pointed out, Adams fruitfully refined a basic tool of the economist, the "law of return and variable costs." "Henry Carter Adams: Critic of *Laissez-Faire*," *Journal of Social Philosophy* 3:244 (April, 1938).

the wasteful, temporary competition. The question, said Adams, was whether society should support an irresponsible extralegal monopoly, or monopoly established by law and managed in the public interest.

The range of industries subject to increasing returns, Adams felt, was relatively narrow, though basic—transportation, telegraph, gas, and water. Regulation should be largely under state rather than federal supervision.

Adams was not sympathetic to state regulating commissions which either attempted to maintain competition among the railroads or had merely advisory functions on the model of that of Massachusetts. But admitting the principle of control by commissions, he said successful operation required that a federal commission complement the state commissions, that pooling contracts be legalized, and that the "commissions be courts of registry and adjudication." He seemed to favor the original French procedure of "territorialization," by which the country was divided into districts and charters granted to private corporations for the exclusive management of railroads within each district. Public interest, he declared, was conserved by direct government control and by the right of repurchase at "an appraisement." But to satisfy the clamor of the French public for more roads, added Adams, the original design was abandoned, and disaster resulted.[27]

Would not government control, whether by factory legislation or regulation of monopoly, cause corruption? Not necessarily. Adams argued that corruption was due to the lack of correlation between the duties assigned to public officials and the functions performed by private individuals, so that the inducement offered varied too widely. Extension

[27] Adams, *Outline of Lectures* (1886 ed.), pp. 64–65.

of the State's administrative functions, manned by an adequate well-paid Civil Service, would restore the harmony between State and private service, for it would bring social distinction, the chance to exercise one's talents, and the pleasure of filling well a responsible position.

Factory legislation and monopoly regulation, however, did not touch the problem of the rights and duties under which work is done. In the midst of the second strike against the Gould railroad system in March, 1886, Adams developed his solution of this serious "social question."

A number of people were so obsessed with the danger of "anarchism" that they began to lean toward a police state as an antidote. In alarm Adams recalled to the American public his own experience in Germany in the days of the "detestable system" of "police surveillance" under Bismarck's Anti-Socialist Laws.

> I did not find it pleasant to be obliged to show a passport before a hotel proprietor would . . . assign me a room. It was a disagreeable necessity imposed upon me that I should look into each morning's paper under the list of books *verboten,* to see which ones in my possession next should be put under lock and key. And I confess to . . . a moderate degree of anger when, as I was quietly whistling upon a street to drive away my melancholy, a policeman touched me on the shoulder with the remark: *Pfeifen wird nicht gestattet* [Whistling is not permitted]. And my capacity for contempt was exhausted when I heard a prominent professor of the greatest university in the world reply to a student, who asked permission to make a special study of the progressive income tax, *Mein Gott! das is aber etwas gefährlich* [My God, that is rather dangerous].[28]

Adams presented his position on labor relations in a solicited newspaper article, "What Do These Strikes

[28] Adams, "Shall We Muzzle the Anarchists?" *Forum,* 1:453 (July, 1886).

Mean?" and he elaborated it at a symposium on the "Labor Problem" at Cornell's recently established Sibley College of Engineering.[29]

The principle underlying the cooperative theory, he declared, was that proprietorship should be widely diffused in order that the benefits of property might be widely diffused. This purpose could be achieved "while the nominal or legal residence of property remains where it is." The student must look beyond the excesses of labor organizations. Viewed historically the labor movement was a step in the further development of individual rights, and harmonized with the basic ideal of Anglo-Saxon institutions, that of equal rights and personal responsibility.

The labor movement marked the attempt to achieve "industrial liberty" as the necessary complement to religious and political liberty. The religious reformation had secured for each man the right to maintain his own opinions in matters spiritual, a right that has naturally grown into the modern doctrine of freedom of thought, speech, and press. The political revolution, which had been realized through the struggle for ministerial responsibility, had secured for men the right of self-government. The Industrial Revolution had as its objective the exercise of social responsibility. In the scheme of petty industry, the regime of tools, the ordinary rights of "personal freedom" secured to men an enjoyment of the fruits of their labor. In great industries, the laborer was dependent upon the owner of machines, of materials, and of places for the opportunity to work. The old theory of liberty, which placed the personal right to acquire property on the same footing as the right to security

[29] Adams's address was published in *Scientific American Supplement*, 22:8861–63 (August 21, 1886).

of life, was no longer applicable to modern society. Those who believed that the law of property had reached the "limit of its evolution" had been compelled to turn their minds toward authority and thus betrayed infidelity to the "claims of a free society."

Since the structure of modern industry, based on machinery, required concentration of capital, it followed that laborers must unite or they would surely get the worst of any bargain. Underlying labor's demands was the "idea" that the laborers had some right of proprietorship in the industry to which they gave their skill and time. This could be realized, he argued, by imposing certain duties upon the holders of property. And this was the purpose of the trade-union movement. Arbitration was the machinery by which responsibilities could be imposed on the legal owners of capital. Tenure and promotion according to civil service rules would give a vested interest in the industry. "If," he wrote, "employees are consulted whether hours of work or the numbers employed shall be reduced, they have secured a right to live in hard times from the fund of capital created by them in flush times." Thus, collective bargaining and the labor contract envisaged a crystallization of a "common law of labor rights," and would ultimately result in the establishment of "Federation in Industries."

Workmen would receive the benefits of industrial partnership without disturbing the existing nominal or legal ownership, and a new law of productive property would arise.

In "Economics and Jurisprudence," a later address (1896), which is reprinted in this volume, he reasserted his faith in a new "proprietary" system. The development of proprietary labor rights would lead to responsibility, for labor would have something at stake in maintaining orderly relations. That workingmen resort to violence and employers call for troops was the result of the fact that labor had nothing to lose under existing arrangements.[30] Thus the underlying purpose or guiding end of the labor movement was opposed to the tyranny of German socialism and was in full harmony with the development of Anglo-Saxon liberty.

Adams's views on state regulation of monopolies and factory legislation, as well as those on "cooperation," coming as they did at a time of hysteria, shocked influential circles. For example, an anonymous editorial in the *Nation* on his address, "Principles that Should Control the Interference of the States in Industries," warned Cornell that Adams was "coquetting with anarchy." The *Independent* declared that the "views which underlay modern socialism are here put in their strongest shape with a moderation which makes them all the more insidious." Henry Sage, Chairman of the Board of Trustees and a prominent benefactor of Cornell, expressed a sharp opinion of "self appointed reformers."[31]

The Cornell address on the "Labor Problem" was especially misunderstood, though it should be noted that Adams innocently contributed to the misunderstanding. The center of national attention at the time was the second strike of the

[30]This sharpening of Adams's position may well have been due to the famous Pullman strike of 1894, sometimes called "Debs' Rebellion," which involved the railroad industry as well as the Pullman Company. For Adams's contemporary view of the strike, see Adams, "The Railway Situation," *Review of Reviews*, 10:186–87 (August, 1894).

[31]Sage, "The Labor Problem," *Scientific American Supplement*, 22:8877 (August 28, 1886).

Interestingly, the outstanding reformer Henry Demarest Lloyd contended that Adams was wrong in holding that the "workmen must work their reforms out between themselves and their employers without invoking the help of the state." Lloyd to Adams, December 6, 1886; copy in Henry D. Lloyd Papers, State Historical Society of Wisconsin (Madison, Wis.).

Knights against Jay Gould's Southwestern Railroad System. Adams, in the address as well as in the newspaper article, accepted at face value the public statements of the striking Knights that they were striking to end arbitrary dismissals and discrimination against the Knights. Adams quoted these statements extensively as indicating that the drift of the labor movement was in line with his notion of labor's proprietary rights. When events revealed that the strike leaders were really interested in a violent "crusade against capital," Adams admitted his error as to the intentions of the leaders of the Knights. Yet he had raised doubts as to his soundness, and his hope to end his "apprenticeship" was at stake. His associate professorship at Cornell had been renewed for another two-year term ending in 1887. Events had taken such a turn that he became alarmed that the prize of a permanent appointment as a full professor might not be his. He appealed to his academic friends for aid. Some of them responded. For example, Richard T. Ely, secretary of the American Economic Association, announced that *Relation of the State to Industrial Action* was a profound study, and that it would be published by the Association. Professor E. R. A. Seligman of Columbia, in a review of the monograph in the scholarly *Political Science Quarterly*, declared,

In this suggestive monograph, the main point that strikes the reader is its essential conservatism. It is the best proof of the fact that an abandonment of *laissez faire* does not connote socialism or anything approaching socialism. Professor Adams expressly and repeatedly shows that the old principle of personal responsibility is instinct with vitality. He believes that the labor problem must be worked on the basis of free contract, and maintains that the state must not control labor relations. This analysis simply results in the demand for factory legislation—which will be denied by no one today—and in the claim for public control over corporate monopolies. . . . If only facts, and not fancies be regarded, it will be seen that the opponents of *laissez faire* are verily the true conservatives.

Adams's students addressed a favorable petition to the board of trustees. However, the Cornell authorities in 1887 postponed selection of a full professor, and with the expiration of Adams's appointment, his connection with Cornell ceased. It should be said that three years later, the trustees, including Sage, unsuccessfully sought to bring Adams back as a full professor.[32]

Meanwhile, Adams had intensified his endeavors to secure a full professorship at Michigan where he taught in alternate terms. The hitherto unpublished letters of Adams to President Angell in the Michigan Historical Collections of the University of Michigan reveal the hard but successful struggle. President Angell had for some time been disturbed about Adams's views. Adams's kind of economics was alien to Angell's traditions. The previous year he had addressed to Adams a series of searching interrogations on such matters as property, inheritance, and socialism. Adams had replied along the lines set forth in his papers. Angell was not satisfied. Adams's second reply of March 15, 1887, is a significant document in the story of academic freedom.

Ithaca, N.Y.
March 15, 1887

Dear Dr. Angell:

I don't think there is any danger of my misunderstanding your letter or the spirit in which it is written. Last year,

[32]Seligman, in "Memorial to Former President Henry C. Adams," *American Economic Review*, 12:405 (September, 1922).

your questions came to me with the shock of a complete surprise, but I am coming to be pretty well accustomed to such expressions now.

You ask if I can help you any more so you can see your way clear to my nomination. I don't see as I can, except it be to suggest that, in my opinion, your point of view in this matter is not the right one. If you make a man's opinions the basis of his election to a professorship, you do, whether you intend it or not, place bonds upon the free movement of his intellect. It seems to me that a Board has two things to hold in view. First, is a man a scholar? Can he teach in a scholarly manner? Is he fair to all parties in the controverted questions which come before him? Second, is he intellectually honest? If these two questions are answered in the affirmative, his influence upon young men cannot be detrimental.

Upon these points, certainly nothing new can be said. I have served for five years as an apprentice and you have had opportunity to know. Or, with regard to the fairness in which topics are presented in the classroom, you have the outline of lectures. My conscious purpose in teaching is twofold. To portray social problems to men as they will find them to be when they leave the University and to lead men to recognize that morality is an everyday affair.

But all this, you will say, is by the point. You say you do not know what my views are on capital and labor. I am not surprised at that for I have intentionally withheld them. No one knows them, and I had made up my mind to keep them to themself until I had worked through my study of the development of industrial society. My reason for such a decision was, that, in my study of social questions I had found myself on all sides of the question. I started as an individualist of the most pronounced type. But my advocacy of it led me to perceive its errors, and my criticisms were formulated before I read any literature of socialism. But when, upon coming into contact with socialistic writers, I found their criticisms were the same as my own, I was for a while carried away with their schemes. But upon further study, I found their plans to be, not only as I thought—impracticable, but contrary to the fundamental principle of English political philosophy, in which I still believed. You can imagine that was not a pleasant condition for one appreciative of logical symmetry. You said a year ago that my views were not logical, that is, that some of my expressions were contradictory to each other. I don't doubt that they appeared so. It seems bad logic to admit the purpose of individualism and the criticism of socialists at the same time. You say now in your letter that I have not worked out my ideas into clear and definite shape. That is true, but I am doing it as fast as I can in my own way. My book upon Pub[lic] Debts is one step in this direction.

But to go back to the development of this subject in my own mind. The illogical position into which my mind had drifted, as the result of the first five years of study, was the occasion of keen intellectual pain; but the sense of the necessity of harmony led me finally to discover a principle which I thought, and still think, adequate to bridge over the chasm between the purpose of individualism and the criticisms of socialism. This principle is the principle of personal responsibility in the administration of all social power, no matter in what shape that power may exist. This principle has given form to our political society; I wish it to be brought over into industrial relations. Its realization will cure the ills of which socialists complain, without curbing or crushing that which is the highest in the individual. I thought, at first, this principle to be so simple that its statement must gain for it quick recognition. But when I tried to make that statement, and work the theory out, I was at once surprised and chagrined to see what a task lay before me. It is useless to deny that the interests of the privileged classes in our civilization is against responsible administration of industrial power. I worked at it for a year, and then came to the conclusion that I did not yet know enough, nor was I sure enough of my position, to make public the thought which had assumed direction of my studies. It was then that I took up the study of Finance and went to work on Pub[lic] Debts. This is the most simple of any of the topics which must be treated as the subject of constructive Economics opened before me; it was also furtherest removed from the points likely to give rise to controversy. I thought I might, perhaps, gain the reputation of a sound thinker so that expressions of views more unusual might attract a candid reading from scholarly men. It has taken a year and a half longer than I had anticipated, and now that it is done seems to have dwarfed in importance.

I do not think this narration will relieve you from embarrassment. I do not see that anything can do that, except a promise on my part to give expression only to orthodox views of social relations. But it has relieved me somewhat and I trust you will consider that an adequate apology. I of course have full confidence in your personal friendship; I only wish you might have equal confidence in my scholarly purposes.

Very sincerely yours,

H. C. Adams

P.S. May I add a postscript, for I am sure it is an unjustifiable pride which kept me from inserting it in the body of my letter. I presume the expression of my views which have given you the greatest solicitude are to be found in the Sibley address [on the "Labor Problem"] of last year, and in the syndicate article which I wrote on the Knights of Labor ["What Do These Strikes Mean?"]. I do not wish to recall anything said, but I am willing to say that these expressions were as unwise as they were unpremeditated. In justice to myself I should say: That the Sibley address was on Friday afternoon and my invitation was on the Wednesday previous. Professor [R. H.] Thurston [Director of Sibley College] said he had been disappointed in his lecturer for the afternoon, that he did not like to postpone the meeting, and that he would like me to open a discussion on the labor problem. He told me, who besides myself would speak and they were all decidedly opposed to any expression of sympathy with the struggle of the Knights then going on. After my opening address, the man against whom I talked, who, it was said, would reply to me, took his hat and left. Others spoke, among them [the new] President [Charles Kendall] Adams, Mr. [Herbert] Tuttle [Professor of the History of Political and Municipal Institutions and of International Law] & Henry Sage. The President was not dogmatical, but did not understand what I tried to say. The others were. My part in the discussion has cost me a professorship, for I do not see how, with the views of Mr. Sage as to the function of a teacher, he can vote for me. It was after the address was made that the talk began, and I thought it then cowardly not to let it be printed, and dishonest to change it. So it went in, as nearly as I could remember as it was given. I think it unfair to judge of my classroom work by this address.

With regard to the syndicate article, I confess myself to

have been deceived by the attitude of the Knights of Labor during their [second] strike on the Gould System, or I should not have written it. In their articles of complaint, they said certain things which I believed to be true, and I thought the men who drew them up had thought the labor problem through to its end, and had made a stand on a principle in harmony with English Liberties. If so, it was time for men of standing to declare themselves. But it turns out that the Knights hit the mark by a chance shot. They did not know what they were about and got whipped as they deserved. The result of this unfortunate venture is, that I believe more strongly than ever in the necessity of scholarship as an element in the solution of this terrible question that is upon us.

Have you seen "The Ind[ustrial] Revolution" by Arnold Toynbee? His death is a loss. The scraps of his lectures and letters [in this posthumous volume] show him to have had much the same purpose as myself in his studies.

Respectfully,

HCA

The upshot was that the Board of Regents of the University of Michigan gave him the appointment in June, 1887, at an initial salary of $2,200. He remained at the University of Michigan to the end of his life.

Backed by a permanent post, Adams sought to expand political economy in the academic world and in the world of affairs. The new interest in industrial and social questions, he said, was one of the means by which society was endeavoring to adjust its legal and ethical structure to the new condition of industry created by the new technology.

The inventor and engineer are in this case the forerunners of the economist, and the task of the economist will not be completed, until the business men learn to draw contracts, and the legislators to pass laws, according to principles that are fundamentally sound, because conformable to the new ways in which business is carried on.[33]

Adams began stressing the study of statistics. "Because reasoning from assumed premises was unable longer to command the confidence of the public . . . students have addressed themselves to the more difficult task of reasoning from the premises which statistics alone can furnish."[34] This emphasis on statistical inquiry was in good part an outgrowth of his contribution to public service as the first statistician of the Interstate Commerce Commission (1887–1911). As such, he played a creative role in the pioneer attempt at national regulation.

The first chairman of this commission was his Johns Hopkins teacher and Michigan colleague, the outstanding student of American constitutional law, Thomas McIntyre Cooley. Chairman Cooley gave Adams his appointment, and Adams made the job a basic part of effective regulation. He firmly believed that no adequate supervision of the railroads could be achieved unless their statistics were controlled. After a twenty-year struggle he won out. The system of uniform standardized accounts, subject to government inspection, which Adams developed for the I.C.C., has since been extended to other utilities and to other jurisdictions.

[33]Adams, "Ten Years of Political Economy in the United States," *Inlander*, 1:24 (March, 1891). For Adams's role in economics at the University of Michigan, see Z. C. Dickinson's "The Department of Economics," in *The University of Michigan*, ed. Wilfred B. Shaw, Part III (Ann Arbor, Mich., 1943), pp. 434–36.

[34]Adams, "Smith's Statistics and Economics" in *Publications of the American Statistical Association* (Boston), new series 1:217 (March, 1889).

Adams became at the same time one of the chief defenders of regulation by commissions. The prime merit of a regulating commission, he declared, was that such a body could focus the varied experiences of independent managers upon a particular question and "select a rule of uniformity best adapted to the aggregate of industries" considered as a unit. The commission's approach for determining the principles of unreasonable discrimination, was not by "philosophic generalization but by . . . investigation and adjudication" of cases. From the opinions expressed upon cases there developed a system of "authoritative rules and established interpretations" which eventually would come to be recognized as a body of administrative law for inland transportation.[35]

To the increasing number of observers who contended after a decade that the I.C.C. had been a failure, Adams pointed out that its shortcomings flowed in good part from Supreme Court decisions stripping it of effective power. The courts, he said, were unduly jealous towards an administrative body clothed with judicial or semijudicial functions. He asserted in 1893 that if the commission was to administer speedy relief to a shipper who was being destroyed by secret contracts or rebates granted to a competitor, its findings in regard to the facts must be final. Otherwise the commission merely increased the difficulty complained of, since for all practical purposes, the commission became just another court from which appeal could be taken. He pointed out that the Supreme Court also denied the commission the right to prescribe reasonable rates, but limited it to setting aside "unreasonable" rates fixed by a company.

[35]Adams, "A Decade of Federal Railway Regulation," *Atlantic Monthly*, 81:437–38 (1898).

Finally, the Court decisions had negated the intention of Congress that the commission prescribe a uniform system of accounts and have the fullest liberty of investigating the books of the corporations and of securing evidence from witnesses. He therefore suggested that Congress strengthen the commission and render its rights so clear that even in jealousy the courts could not misunderstand them. Control of railways by commissions was the truly conservative method of control.

If it succeeds, we may look for a solution of all the vexed industrial problems in harmony with the fundamental principles of English liberty. If it fails, there is nothing for the future of our civilization but the tyranny of socialism.[36]

In spite of the discouragement Adams worked strenuously to have set up a Bureau of Statistics and Accounts armed with the powers that could realize the idea of the commission. Such a bureau was eventually established by the Hepburn Act of 1906, which removed a number of the weaknesses in the old law. Adams's title was changed from "Statistician to the Commission," to "In Charge of the Division of Statistics and Accounts."

From the beginning, Adams called for comprehensive legislation to provide for reports and regulation by the commission of all the agencies of transportation including water carriers. Adams especially demanded that the commission control the accounts of all corporations and other concerns directly interested in railway traffic, particularly the construction companies. Certainly, he said, investors have a legitimate right to demand that public control over corporate accounts be carried as "far as to guaranty to investors

[36] Adams, "Interstate Commerce Act—Discussion," in *Publications of the Michigan Political Science Association* (Ann Arbor, Mich.), 1:143 (May, 1893).

the integrity of the statements upon which the value of their property depends." Speaking more broadly, he declared in 1892 that government could not undertake the "exercise of paternalism to the extent of protecting individuals in their investment," but it could determine in some degree the conditions under which investments were made and provide for the exposure of facts in such a manner that the purchase of railway stocks would become less speculative than it was at that time.[37]

But it was the consumer interest that must be paramount. Adams's long insistence that the physical valuation of company property be considered basic led to the formulation of a more tangible and effective basis for arriving at rates along the lines of "original cost." He went further, arguing that since the rates set must be high enough to permit the survival of roads operating under inferior conditions, the roads more favorably situated would enjoy a tremendous gain. Since the differences in earnings were in part due to social conditions, such as better natural routes, equity demanded that excess returns or surplus profits—at least a good part of them—accruing to such roads should be turned over to the state.[38]

[37]Adams, "A Bureau of Railway Statistics and Accounts," *Independent*, 44:1384–85 (October 6, 1892). Adams, *Eighth Annual Report on The Statistics of Railways in the United States*, 1895 (Washington, 1896), p. 102.

Adams also stressed the fact that such control over accounts would result in widespread confidence in railroad securities, and this, in turn, would tend to check those "violent movements of the industrial pendulum between periods of unreasonable activity and periods of equally unreasonable depression to which modern business is exposed." Adams, "The Administrative Supervision of Railways under the Twentieth Section of the Act to Regulate Commerce," *Quarterly Journal of Economics*, 22:375–76 (May, 1908).

[38]Adams, *Commercial Valuation of Railway Operating Property in the United States, 1904*, United States Bureau of the Census Bulletin No. 21 (Washington, 1905), p. 8. Adams, "Valuation of Public Service Utilities," in *Publications of the American Economic Association*, 3d series (Cambridge, Mass.), 11:193 (April, 1910).

Adams applied his philosophy of control to other large-scale industries. The corporate form of organization, he declared, had intensified the monopoly problem, and through its aggregate power further threatened to corrupt democratic institutions. The limited liability privilege had proved the source of vast public mischief. The corporation violated the principle that responsibility should be commensurate with the liberty enjoyed. Managers could and did engage in vast speculation and reckless activities for their own profit. The risk, however, rested on other members of the community, such as investors, or on the community as a whole. This irresponsibility of corporate management contributed to panics and crises.

Adams felt that although competition might control industries when they were made up of small and numerous units, it was ineffective when these units became large and relatively few. Similarly, intercorporate competition was essentially different in its operation and results from interpersonal competition.

> Not only has the industrial power of our day, generated by the organization of labor and extensive use of machinery, fallen under the control of corporations, but these corporations assert for themselves most of the rights conferred on individuals by the law of private property, and apply to themselves a social philosophy true only of a society composed of individuals who are industrial competitors.

The remedy, he was convinced, was certainly not the abolition of limited liability. Rather, he suggested in 1894, the corporate form be limited to "natural monopolies" or industries of "increasing returns." In fact, such industries should be compelled to take the corporate form; as corporations, they should be required to make reports which would enable the government acting under rules prescribed by law, to direct their policy, and control their administration. Holding a corporation which performed a public service to account, as an officer of the government was held to account, could not be considered socialistic, he contended. He advocated the use of taxation, especially corporate income taxation for natural monopolies, on the basis of his conception of capital as a social product. Since the value of the "monopoly" increased with the growth of society, "the increment of earnings is largely an unearned increment to the corporation and should be directed through the machinery of taxation to the benefit of the citizens from which it accrues." All other businesses should be subject to inquiry, though not to control, in order to determine whether or not they "should be refused the liberty of incorporation or be required to assume corporate form."[39]

In 1899, recognizing that the states individually were unable to cope with "artificial monopoly," because of the scale of modern business, he proposed, at the famous Chicago Anti-Trust Conference, that the states act together to set up an interstate organization of statistical inquiry and grant it adequate authority for effective prosecution of its investigations.[40]

Adams also stressed as an instrument of control of the corporation the adequate education of its future executives. This he expounded explicitly at the turn of the century as he

[39]Adams, "Suggestions for a System of Taxation," *Publications of the Michigan Political Science Association* (Ann Arbor, Mich.), 1, no. 2, 60 (May, 1894). "Publicity and Corporate Abuses," *ibid.*, pp. 116–20.

[40]Adams, "A Statement of the Trust Problem," in *Chicago Conference on Trusts* (Chicago, 1900), p. 41.

Adams also contended by 1898 that for its effective functioning non-monopolistic business required ever-increasing governmental statistical services in order to reduce the uncertainty that surrounded business transactions as business grew more complex.

viewed the rising demand for commercial education as a response to the growth in number and size of corporations, especially those in manufacturing. He pointed out that the dominant executive, whom he called the "corporate financier," combined the roles of promoter, business manager, and administrator of social power. Among the subjects requisite for success in the first two roles, was "sufficient acquaintance with mathematics and the science of statistics and accounts to test not only the success of his own administration, but to judge of the general trend of industry in the business world." The third function, Adams frankly stated, was a subject of controversy for here entered the public interest.

> In a sense every great industrial enterprise is clothed with a quasi-public interest. This is due in part to the fact that the public as consumers are interested in economy of administration, but primarily to the fact that a business organization is a depository of social power, and on this account cannot be safely administered independently of social considerations. Even from the point of view of the corporation, which, it must be remembered, enjoys perpetual existence, it must be conceded that the highest success can only be obtained when the administrator of the corporation is consciously influenced by other than business interests.

Thus, the appropriate education of the executive must include more than those studies which temper the imagination and those investigations and researches which provide an understanding of physical conditions and mechanical forces. It must also comprise a sufficient amount of history, economics, and ethics to enable him to appreciate the part which corporations play in modern life and, in addition, the fundamental rights and duties of the people with whom his position would bring him into business relations.[41]

[41] Adams, "The Corporate Financier and Commercial Education," *Michigan Alumnus*, 9:93–94 (December, 1902).

In these manifold ways Adams showed a constructive appreciation of the fact that the "corporation problem" embraces most of the significant industrial problems of modern times.

Out of his last major venture in public service came another fruitful suggestion. In 1913–14 and during the academic year 1915–16, Adams served as Adviser to the Commission on Unification of Accounts for the Government Railways of China. This led him to extend his jurisprudence to the one field he had heretofore left "completely at the mercy of purely commercial efforts"—foreign economic relations and especially investment in undeveloped countries. He pointed out that no school of economic thought provided a method for handling the problem, which, like the labor question, called for constructive diplomacy. Adams's proposal of an international commission of competent men, including representatives of China, to supervise the current operations and future construction of the Chinese railways, contained the germ of a development that today holds much promise for the peace of the world.[42]

In the field that Adams had originally made his specialty, "Public Finance," he was on the whole somewhat less adventurous than elsewhere. But even in this field his "organic viewpoint" proved fertile as he developed the principles of public finance in their manifold relations to social, political, and economic progress. With his fellow spirit E. R. A. Seligman he pioneered in making the subject an important branch of economics both in the academic world and in public affairs. His *Public Debts* (1887) was the first American work of distinction on the subject, and *The Science of*

[42]Adams, "International Supervision over Foreign Investments," *American Economic Review*, Vol. 10 (March, 1920), Supplement pp. 58–67.

Finance (1898) was a landmark in its field. Its originality, power of analysis, and maturity of thought were universally acknowledged. His notable work with the Michigan Tax Commission, particularly in connection with valuation for tax purposes of the Michigan railroads, played an important role in the recognition by public bodies of the value of trained economists.

Adams early recognized that Treasury operations affected the economy. Thus in 1888 in discussing the danger of the government having a surplus revenue, he pointed out that if government accumulated a substantial surplus, that is, hoarded it, "it would tend to bring about a stringent money market, and would probably precipitate a commercial crisis." In the First World War, Adams proposed a scheme for the prevention of wartime inflation of which the last has not yet been heard. Recognizing on the one hand that inflation must be controlled and on the other hand that farmers, wage earners, and producers of war goods might require increased returns or prices to mobilize effectively the country's resources for the war effort, Adams proposed that such increases be paid in the form of a guaranty, in government bonds redeemable only at the end of the war.[43]

Adams's work throughout was characterized by a broad humanism. This emerges most strikingly in his address on the "Social Ministry of Wealth," which Adams delivered before a number of important institutions in 1892–1893. This address dealt with the problem of the utilization of leisure. Businessmen would not retire lacking as they did any other

[43]Adams, "Surplus Financiering," in *National Revenues*, ed. Albert Shaw (Chicago, 1888), p. 45. Adams, "Borrowing As a Phase of War Financing," *Annals of the American Academy of Political and Social Science* (Philadelphia), 75:23–30 (January, 1918).

passion but that of accumulation; this could be alleviated if men of wealth would use part of their fortunes to provide for the arts in the colleges, for then students would learn to appreciate the amenities and social pleasures of life, without eliminating the necessary spirit of business enterprise. Exposed to the best in music and art, they would introduce a spirit of the beautiful which would ultimately change the character of the American people. In such ways the wonderful facilities for the production of wealth, which characterize the nineteenth century, would be diverted from the service of "degrading ambition and made to perform the social function to which the logic of history declares them to be called."[44]

Adams's humanistic outlook was indeed so genuine and attractive that it drew students among whom were to be such outstanding social scientists as the historian James Franklin Jameson, the political scientist J. Allen Smith, the sociologist Charles Horton Cooley, the economist David Friday. But Adams's influence reached beyond his own students. He was among the first to emphasize systematically the pivotal role of the corporate institution including its importance as an instrument of capital accumulation. His emphasis on accounting and statistics as instruments of social control was far-reaching and fruitful. The United States Bureau of Corporations and its successors, the Federal Trade Commission and the Securities Exchange Commission, are only a few of the results. His law of increasing returns, crude and incomplete as he admitted his formulation to be, remains a central point in discussions of

[44]Adams, "The Social Ministry of Wealth," *International Journal of Ethics*, 4:188 (January, 1894). He was on the journal's editorial board, 1893–1914.

monopoly. His emphasis on the role of technology and especially on that of the Industrial Revolution, whose "end was not yet in sight," promises to continue to supply a powerful rationale of "conservative reform" as against revolution. His powerful notion of "proprietary rights" became so common that its origin was lost. Most forceful was his conception of raising the ethical plane of competition. This exercised a considerable influence on the younger economists and the public and became the underlying intellectual basis of ameliorative legislation in the development of a labor code and a code of business conduct. In the course of time it was expanded much beyond the limits he had specified. Such things, considered by Adams paternalistic and mistaken charity, as public housing and government insurance for workmen, have since become imbedded in the plane of competition. But then Adams, like most of his generation, was impressed with the spectral warning of the Malthusian doctrine of population.

Similarly, in the area of business conduct, Congress over the years in its enactment of the telling series of prohibitions against unfair competitive practices has acted on Adams's philosophy that these laws do not abandon or abridge competition but establish a moral plane for competition.

Society, the living, growing organism, was Adams's ultimate concern, and state action, like industrial or ethical activity, was a function of the whole. "The great problem of the present day," he said in 1885, "is properly to correlate public and private activity so as to preserve harmony and proportion between the various parts of organic society." On behalf of the "moral dignity of man," he worked to achieve those legal and social conditions which would bring into "natural and spontaneous exercise the tremendous force of moral character."[45]

This strong note of social morality underlay the address at Johns Hopkins in 1915 in which he envisaged, for some time to come, the "continuous triumph of the capitalistic organization of industry" based on machinery and, with it, the wage system, collective bargaining, the world market, and the corporation.

The tendencies of the future must be more and more toward the complete realization of an industrial democracy, and . . . the art of living adjusted to the requirements of a moral control over materialistic concerns must be a democratized art. Not that democracy is a thing of beauty, although much poetry, and good poetry, has been written under its inspiration, but that the failure to attain social and industrial democracy will prove to be the beginning of the end of industrial efficiency and national power. An appreciation of equity as defined by democracy and a conception of responsibility as reflected from social morality provides the only way for averting the prostitution of materialistic possibilities to ignoble ends and the consequent debauchment of the race.

The price of achievement was not cheap, he proclaimed, for the humanistic democracy was not one of mere equality. It involved the successful education of the people in its ideals.

Democracy as an ideal is devoid of character. As John Stuart Mill so justly observes there is an equality of degradation as well as of excellence. . . . If the kind of democracy which the people choose bears the fruit of high ideals; if it realizes some of the finer things of human relations; if it hammers out a standard of dignity and of

[45]Statement of Adams quoted in R. T. Ely, "Report of the Organization of the American Economic Association," in *Publications of the American Economic Association* (Baltimore), 1, no. 1, 21 (March, 1886).

Adams, Introduction to Jane Addams, *et. al., Philanthropy and Social Progress,* New York, 1893), p. VII. The volume comprised lectures at the School of Applied Ethics, of which Adams was dean.

courtesy for national, social and personal evaluation of conduct and attainment, the stress and storm of past endeavor will have been amply justified.[46]

We can still profit from his wisdom as we seek to do for our generation what he did for his: help check disintegrating tendencies and reinvigorate a sense of mutual dependence essential to healthy individualism.

[46]Adams, "The Present Significance of Academic Instruction," *Johns Hopkins University Circular,* 34:553–54 (June, 1915). At this time Johns Hopkins awarded him an LL.D., a degree which he had received previously from Wisconsin and Grinnell.

Note on the Text

HENRY CARTER ADAMS's essay, "Relation of the State to Industrial Action," is reprinted from *Publications of the American Economic Association,* Volume I, Number 6 (January, 1887), pages 465–549.

"Economics and Jurisprudence," the other of his essays included in this volume, was his Presidential Address before the American Economic Association, delivered on December 28, 1896, in Baltimore. It is reprinted from *American Economic Association, Economic Studies,* Volume II, Number 1 (February, 1897), pages 1–48. The discussion of the paper on the following morning is included. The address was also printed in Schmoller's *Jahrbuch für Gesetzgebung, Verwaltung und Volkswirstschaft im Deutschen Reich,* 22 Jahrgang, Heft 4 (1898), pages 1360–79. This does not include the discussion, but the translator, Professor Ernst von Halle, gave the substance of it in an illuminating commentary: "Nachwort des Übersetzers," *ibid.,* pages 1379–86.

The notes added to the present reprinting of the text for the most part supply relevant clarifying information on matters that Adams in his essays naturally treated as common knowledge to his generation or to his original audience of professional economists—matters, however, which are less familiar to the general reader of today. For similar reasons descriptions have been supplied of the discussants of his address (the second essay).

Relation of the State to Industrial Action

Let the State be considered as subordinate to the people; but let everything else be subordinate to the State.

MR. JUSTICE WILSON, 1792

The greatest part of mankind may be divided into two classes; that of SHALLOW *thinkers, who fall short of the truth, and that of* ABSTRUSE *thinkers, who go beyond it. The latter class are by far the most uncommon, and I may add, by far the most useful and valuable. They suggest hints, at least, and start difficulties, which they want, perhaps, skill to pursue, but which may produce fine discoveries, when handled by men who have a more just way of thinking. At worst, what they say is uncommon; and if it should cost some pains to comprehend it, one has, however, the pleasure of hearing something that is new. An author is little to be valu'd, who tells us nothing but what we can learn from every coffee-house conversation.*

DAVID HUME ["OF COMMERCE," IN *Political Discourses* (EDINBURGH, 1752), P. 1]

PREFACE The following essay is a revision, and an extension, of a paper read before The Constitution Club and The Institute of Social Science, both of the City of New York, and published by the first-mentioned society under the title, "Principles that Should Control the Interference of the States in Industries." Its appearance in its present form is due to the fact that more applications have been made for the original address than could be supplied, and this was interpreted as an expression of interest in the topic. It is of course impossible to treat at all adequately so important a subject as "The Relation of the State to Industrial Action" in a single monograph. Still no serious misunderstanding is apprehended, except possibly in connection with the explanation of prevalent corruption in municipal administration; and upon this point it may be well to say, that the purpose of this essay is not so much to expound a final theory respecting the evils of local government, as to leave the impression that the problem of local government is but a subordinate part of the great social problem.

INTRODUCTION

IN HIS LATEST contribution to the discussion of social topics, Mr. Spencer has collated, for the benefit of his readers, a long list of acts passed by Parliament pertaining to industrial affairs. These enactments he regards as an invasion of the domain of personal liberty, because an encroachment upon the "*régime* of contract." He conceives it as beyond question that "Government is begotten of aggression and by aggression," and for that reason deprecates the willingness on the part of legislators to pass laws regulating the processes of production, or extending the administrative duties of the state. His idea seems to be that the most perfect society which it is possible to realize under given conditions, must emerge from the struggle for individual existence under "voluntary coöperation." All this, as is well known, is the doctrine of *laissez-faire*, presented it is true, in a clear and powerful manner, yet presented without modification or apology. That Mr. Spencer would not dissent from such an interpretation of his four articles, published under the title of *The Man* versus *the State*,[1] is shown by the severity of the implied censure which he visits upon the Cobden Club, for having awarded its prize in 1880 to an essay which declared, that "the truth of Free Trade is clouded over by the *laissez-faire* fallacy."

These articles by Mr. Spencer are most interesting and instructive, and much which they contain seems to me to be true. Ignorant legislation is certainly criminal legislation.[2] Laws which rest upon the assumption that government is *in loco parentis* to its subjects, will never witness the development of a people of manly and independent intelligence. The homely maxim that every tub must stand on its own bottom, as also the more ambitious one that every man is the center of his own universe, suggests sound social truths which legislators cannot afford to disregard. "The intrusion of family-ethics into the ethics of the State," by which philanthropy becomes compulsory and misfortune establishes a claim, is illogical to say the least, and will probably result in harm.[3] Nor is anyone more ready to admit than myself, that laws which purpose to supplement the income of laborers by state aid, will surely result in the

[1][Herbert Spencer, *The Man* versus *the State* (New York, 1884), p. 44. *Editor's note.*]

[2]*The Man* versus *the State*, p. 47.

[3]*Ibid.*, p. 66.

decrease of wages, a conclusion which is amply supported by the history of the English poor-laws during the last century.[4] And especially pertinent does it appear to me to accept the ultimate effects rather than the immediate results of legislation as the final test of its wisdom, for it is a truth too often forgotten that laws make up the artificial environment to which society in its development must conform.[5]

And yet, notwithstanding the many truths contained in this interesting discussion, its main conclusions are regarded as untenable by many whose intellectual discernment is at least respectable. It is by no means universally admitted, even among the studious, that the power of government, which properly interpreted is but the authoritative expression of the will of society, should be more sparingly used as society becomes more complex; nor does it pass without question that the best possible results will in all cases follow "voluntary coöperation" under the "*régime* of contract." Indeed there are many men who presume to think a higher code of morality may be realized in business affairs than is imposed by the unregulated workings of the law of supply and demand. Such claims as these are, of course, a distinct denial of the finality of Mr. Spencer's philosophy of social relations, and consequently of the completeness of the analysis upon which it rests. But it is not my purpose to enter upon a critical analysis of this philosophy. Such a task should certainly have been begun with a frank acknowledgement of the indebtedness of the world to the author of this system. The attention of the reader has been drawn to these latest expressions of Mr. Spencer merely for the purpose of showing that, in the mind of the great English

[4] *Ibid.*, p. 22.
[5] *Ibid.*, pp. 23–24.

philosopher at least, the question of the relation of government to industries is a question of great practical importance. Indeed, its bearing upon current affairs is so direct, that all men of thought desire not only to have an opinion, but a reason for their opinion.

Yet it seems hardly necessary to resort to such a measure for the purpose of emphasizing the importance of the theme treated in this essay; for, in the entire range of social and political problems, there are but few which do not, either directly or indirectly, touch upon the power and ability of the government to control industrial action. The railroad problem, for example, has in this country passed beyond the stage at which the right of legal control is contested. That point was settled by the interpretation of the courts on the "granger laws,"[6] and the only question which at present remains has to do with the manner in which the needed control may be successfully exercised. Education is now quite generally regarded as a proper object for the care of government, and its support as a proper source of public expenditure. It is true that the same phase of this problem is not presented to all people. The English are inquiring how to establish secondary education to the best advantage, the people of this country, on the other hand, having deter-

[6] [The Supreme Court in *Munn vs. Illinois* (1876), upheld as constitutional an act of the legislature of Illinois providing for the fixing of maximum charges for the storage of grain in warehouses in Chicago. This decision also validated state legislation fixing railroad rates. The railroads fought the acts on the ground that they violated the clause of the Fourteenth Amendment that reads that no state should "deprive any person of life, liberty, or property, without due process of law, nor deny to any person within its jurisdiction equal protection of the laws."

These acts have been generally attributed to the farmers' organization, The National Order of the Patrons of Husbandry, commonly known as the Grange, of which the members were called "Grangers." Recent scholarship, however, has called attention to the influence also of disaffected business groups. *Editor's note.*]

mined upon the general principles according to which that grade of education should be managed, are turning their attention to technical education, but in neither case is there serious objection to the appropriation of public moneys for such purposes. Or to speak of social problems and labor agitations, we find the sentiment of the great majority of people whose lives are touched by these questions to be largely colored by the thought that somehow governmental agencies are to cure the evils of which complaint is so justly made. Consider for a moment the varied and extensive demands which self-appointed representatives of the laborer's interests make upon government. The government is to build houses for men; the government is to strike bargains for men; the government is to make play for men; the government is to find work for men; indeed, all that men want done, or think they want done, they want, or think they want, the government to do. And it would but strengthen the impression thus gained were we to consider with care the systematic plans of state socialists for revolutionizing industrial affairs.

How may we properly regard such a tendency in public thought? It will add somewhat to my sense of intellectual liberty in making reply to this question, though it may perhaps be unnecessary, if I say, that the opinions expressed throughout this essay are personal opinions, and should not be regarded as representative in character. A new school of thought must of necessity present a less solid front than an established school. Speaking then for myself, I may say, that I sympathize most profoundly with the apprehension expressed by Mr. Spencer in his doleful articles. It is certainly true that much of current legislation enfolds within itself the seeds of a "coming slavery," and that the confidence reposed by unthinking men in the agencies of government springs from the natural optimism of the human mind, rather than from a careful analysis of what the government is. But our escape from the pernicious consequences of such a tendency will not be found in the continued proclamation of a negative philosophy. The only scholarly course lies in subjecting social and industrial relations to a deeper analysis than is presented by those who submit superficial plans of reform. Or, again, it may even be admitted that government is a weak and inefficient thing, obedient to the nod and beck of private interests. But it does not follow from such an admission that a wise man will knowingly render government yet weaker, or more corrupt and more inefficient, by continuing to preach the illogical doctrine of *laissez-faire*. It is at the instance of such suggestions as these that my own thought parts company with the trend of opinion which passes under the name of English economy.

The facts in the case are these: There is at the present time a growing clamor for more government, and, with manhood suffrage, such a clamor will surely secure that which it demands. But government is not a simple or a homogeneous thing. The extension of its functions may mean the extension of any of the three departments into which its powers are necessarily divided, namely: the judicial, the administrative, or the legislative department; or it may result in changing the balance of the powers distributed between the various grades of authority: the Federal government, the State government, and the minor civil divisions. It seems, then, there are several ways in which this demand for more government may be supplied, and in view of the fact that the social workings of public authority are very different according to the nature of the authority, or the center from which it is exercised, and in view of the further fact that the preaching of a philosophy of negations is powerless to quiet the clamor to which existing social evils have given rise, it seems but common sense for men of mental discernment to seek to direct the extension of public authority. This is equivalent to saying that the subject of this essay is pertinent to the times.

This same thought may be presented in another and perhaps a clearer light. It is fact which politicians visit with reproach upon economists, that men who received their education previous to 1860, and who came from college believing in free commercial intercourse as in a new gospel, have, with their maturer years, felt obliged to confess the optimism of their youth to have been a mistake. But in reality there is nothing remarkable in such a fact when it is remembered that the free trade of that day was but a logical conclusion from the dim and uncertain premises of Bastiat and the Manchester school of economists.[7] For it was found

[7][The term "Manchester School" was derisively applied by the German Historical School to what was considered to be the *laissez-faire* position of the English classical political economy as popularized by the leaders of England's great manufacturing center of Manchester.

Adams's usage was along the lines of the definition of his friend E. J. James, of the Wharton School, of the University of Pennsylvania. "The term Manchester party was applied to a wing of . . . (the absolute free-trade school) composed mostly of practical men, who were instrumental in bringing about the great revolution in England's commercial policy, which, beginning with the abolition of the corn laws in 1846, ended with the free trade tariff of 1860. They were opposed to any governmental interference in economic matters, and demanded unlimited competition in every department of industrial life. As a party they have opposed all legislation in favor of the laboring classes, such as factory laws, postal savings banks, etc. For a time they had everything their own way, but have already lost their hold on the public mind." James, "History of Political Economy," in *Cyclopaêdia of Political Science, Political Economy, and of the Political History of the United States,* ed. by John J. Lalor, Vol. 3 (Chicago, 1884), p. 246. *Editor's note.*]

by these men, in the actual management of business affairs, that the premises which as students they had accepted were not of universal application. It was observed, for example, that the tyranny of corporations, which grew naturally from conditions of "industrial freedom," was as grievous as any tyranny ever established by government agency. In this respect, at least, the theory "that Liberty is the fairest of social Harmonies"[8] did not work as their professors had promised. Since, however, political economy had been pursued by them as a mixture of logic and philosophy, rather than as a phase of social development, they did not possess that habit of mind which easily discriminates in the application of principles. It followed as a matter of course that they abandoned free trade. Such is believed to be the mental history of many men of influence in the United States.

But such a surrender of the doctrine of free trade, though serious enough in itself, is of slight importance when compared with the tendency of which it is a specific illustration. The most unfortunate consequence of so vicious a method of education in economics is found in the fact that the collapse of faith in the sufficiency of the philosophy of *laissez-faire*, has left the present generation without principles adequate for the guidance of public affairs. We are now passing through a period of interregnum in the authoritative control of economic and governmental principles. This is indeed cause for grave solicitude, for never were there more difficult problems demanding solution than at the present time, and never were men so poorly equipped for the accomplishment of such a task as are those upon whom these questions are being forced. Herein lies the especial pertinency of the

[8][Frédéric Bastiat, *Harmonies of Political Economy*, trans. from the 3d ed. of the French by Patrick James Sterling, (2d ed.; Edinburgh, 1877), p. 447. *Editor's note.*]

topic considered in this essay. Principles of action we must have, for nothing is so mischievous as the attempted solution of great questions on the basis of immediate interests alone. An erroneous principle, indeed, is better than no principle at all, for it can at least secure some degree of harmony in social affairs. The problem may be stated in a word, as follows: The authority of English economy is shattered beyond recovery; can a truer system of economic thought gain control over the American mind?

ANALYSIS OF THE DOCTRINE OF LAISSEZ-FAIRE

It is impossible, in any discussion upon the proper extent and nature of state functions, to evade the necessity of granting the doctrine of *laissez-faire* a rehearing. No doctrine could have gained such a respectable following except it contained some truth, and it is wise to search for that truth. But of more importance than this, it is against the assumptions of this doctrine that the theory of extended state functions is urged, and for that reason it is natural to expect its analysis will suggest some rules for directing the action of government. That system of thought known as *laissez-faire* has been termed vague, elusive and indefinite; but such expressions are quite incorrect. Indeed, its great influence over the minds of men is largely due to the compactness with which it may be presented, and to the logical form of which its statement is capable. "When those who have been called the *laisser-faire* school have attempted any definite limitation of the province of government," says Mr. [John Stuart] Mill, "they have usually restricted it to the protection of person and property against force and fraud."[9]

[9]*Principles of Political Economy,* Book V, ch. XI, sec. 1.

From this it appears that, in speaking of the claims of *laissez-faire*, we are dealing with a rule laid down for the control of all matters of government, and have to do with "permanent and universal principles of human nature," only so far as we undertake to explain the basis upon which it is conceived to rest.

But this rule which places the government outside all positive direction in industrial affairs may be held in either of two ways. It may be accepted as a premise of universal application to which all legislation must conform, or it may be regarded merely as a maxim, though a maxim with presumption always in its favor. It need hardly be remarked that Bastiat, who mistakes satire for argument, and whose easy writing has been frequently accepted for clear thinking, stands as the representative of his first theory of interpretation. He does not carry his analysis far enough to distinguish between competition as a principal of action, and *laissez-faire* as a dogma for the guidance of government; but defining competition as freedom from restraint, and freedom from restraint as liberty, he conceives all the complicated questions of society to have been asked and answered when he exclaims: "Who so base as to be a slave!" It is such reasoning as this, reasoning which confuses the student by confounding realities with fancies, that is in large degree responsible for the ineffectiveness of economic teachings.

It does not, however, seem necessary to dwell long upon the extreme statement of the dogma of *laissez-faire*. Practical men have expressed a decided unwillingness to accept a premise which precludes the possibility of discussing many problems of current interest. They desire to decide according to observed results, rather than on the basis of an assumed premise which admits of one conclusion only. Nor would it be right to say that all economists, who are properly regarded as members of the English school, maintain the doctrine of non-interference in its extreme form. Thus Mr. Mill follows the statement of his definition, which I have given above, with the remark that it presents a rule to which strict adherence is impossible, for "it excludes some of the most indispensable and unanimously recognized of duties of government;"[10] but when he proceeds to mention these exceptions, he does not go very far beyond the simple rule laid down. Professor [John Elliot] Cairnes, also, after a critical analysis, concludes that the doctrine of *laissez-faire* establishes no rule of scientific pretensions, although in his opinion it is one to which government should in the main conform. It seems to have been the purpose of Professor Cairnes, as shown in his writings, to turn the current of economic thought back to Ricardo, and, avoiding certain mistakes which he believed others to have made, to develop from the Ricardian doctrines a more consistent and truer line of thought. It is for this reason that his views upon the scientific pretension of *laissez-faire* are of much importance.

In proceeding to argue this point, he says:

> I must ask you, in the first place to note what this doctrine of *laissez-faire*, if it is to be taken as a scientific principle, really means. The implied assertion, as I understand it, is this: that, taking human beings as they are, in the actual state of moral and intellectual development they have reached; taking account, further, of the physical conditions with which they are surrounded in the world; lastly, accepting the institution of private property as understood and maintained in most modern states—the promptings of self-interest will lead individuals, in all that range of their conduct which has to do with their material well-being, spontaneously

[10] [*Ibid. Editor's note.*]

to follow that course which is most for their own good and for the good of all. Such is the assertion with which we have now to deal; and you will see at once that it involves the two following assumptions: first, that the interests of human beings are fundamentally the same—that which is most for my interest is also most for the interest of other people; and secondly, that individuals know their interests in the sense in which they are coincident with the interests of others, and that, in the absence of coercion, they will, in this sense, follow them.[11]

This is without doubt a fair statement of the question at issue. If these two propositions are capable of substantial proof, there is no escape from the practical conclusion that society will realize the best of possible results from the unregulated freedom of individual action but if, on the other hand, either of these propositions are found to be in error, we must abandon at least the universality of the rule of non-interference as a premise of public legislation. It may perhaps be admitted that fundamentally, and in the long run of two or three generations, the interests of all members of society are the same; although, as Professor Cairnes himself remarks, this should not be confounded with the statement that class interests are identical. It is true that society is organic and not mechanical, and that each part suffers with the refusal or inability of any other part to perform its ordinary functions. This thought is readily admitted by even the most extreme of socialists and is made by them the apology for much which they advocate in favor of extending the duties of the state.

But the second proposition cannot be admitted as of universal application. It is not true that, when a man advances his own interests or what he believes to be his own interests, he thereby necessarily advances the interests of

[11] *Essays in Political Economy* [New York, 1873], pp. 244–45.

society. This may be the case and again it may not. It seems hardly necessary to illustrate at length a fact which finds continual proof in the ordinary experiences of men's lives. The entire railroad history of this country, as of every country which has endeavored to realize in construction and management the doctrine of restricted governmental control, serves to illustrate how false is such a claim. The interests of construction companies, for example, have led to the creation of twice as much railroad property in the United States as the needs of the country require. This is a misapplication of capital, a misdirection of industrial energy, and can have no other result than to obstruct healthful growth. Yet the construction companies have made it pay. Or, if we turn to consider the management of such railroad lines as are now built, we see that this excess of railroad property necessitates the adoption of false principles for adjusting tariffs. The management of the grain elevators at Buffalo is railroad management in miniature. As stated by a special committee of the Assembly of New York in 1880, there were at Buffalo thirty-four elevators, of which twelve only were needed to do the work of elevating. "It makes no difference," says the report, "what elevator does the work, all get their respective shares of the money earned. One of these elevators has not been used in twenty years, and many of them, according to the testimony, were built for the sole purpose of coming into and receiving a share in the pool."[12]

The same principle that useless property must be paid for, is found in the management of smaller circles of industry. The Wall-paper Association pays to the owner of a

[12]Report of the Special Committee on Railroads [Appointed under a Resolution of the Assembly (of the State of New York), February 28, 1879], Albany, N.Y., 1880, p. 16.

paper-mill on Long Island the sum of $25,000 a year for not running a mill. It is said, though for this I only have newspaper authority, that Mr. [Joseph] Chamberlain, the English statesman, receives payment each year for not sending screws to this country. Or if we turn our attention to workingmen's unions, we find that they administer the apprentice rules in such a manner as to tend to establish within their order an aristocracy of labor, thus decreasing product and in consequence the fund from which all labor must be paid. These illustrations were brought to our notice, not for the purpose of leading to a discussion of the policy of pooling, but rather to enforce the truth that there exists a necessary antagonism between the actions of men when directed by personal motives, and their action when made to conform to the social interests. Even Bastiat recognized the "anti-social" interest of the producer, and for that reason took the interest of the consumer as the true test of right action.[13]

But I cannot think this the most satisfactory manner of exposing the fundamental error in the philosophy of *laissez-faire.* It was said above that the strength of this doctrine lay in the simplicity of its statement, and in the logical form of which its argument is capable; but a careful student, so far from being deceived by this, will rather be assisted in detecting any mistake with which the argument is chargeable. It is evident that the second of the propositions accepted from Professor Cairnes, is the minor premise of a syllogism of which the first proposition serves as a major. The formal statement then of this syllogism would be as follows:

Major premise. All human interests are the same.

[13]*Sophisms of the Protective Policy* [trans. from the 2d French ed. by Mrs. D. J. McCord, with an Introductory Letter by Francis] Lieber [New York, 1884], p. 28.

Minor premise. Each man knows his own interest, and if left to himself, will follow it.

Conclusion. The best possible form of social relations will emerge from the unrestricted play of industrial freedom.

We need not trouble ourselves to criticise the wording of this conclusion, or to inquire what is intended by the expression "industrial freedom," for the argument has gone astray before the conclusion is reached. Indeed, it disregards the most elementary of the rules of logic, for the words used do not bear the same meaning in all parts of syllogism. Thus the major premise contemplates the fundamental or the ultimate interests of men, while in the minor premise it is the immediate interests that are brought to view. But it is a fact with which men are painfully familiar, that even in their personal affairs, they are prone to sacrifice their ultimate interests for their immediate pleasure, and that the motives which control their actions are strong in a ratio inversely to the remoteness of the pleasure to be gained or the pain to be warded off. How then can it be reasonably concluded that the social interest, which is usually the remote interest of the individual, will be in the highest degree served by granting unobstructed play of industrial freedom? There must be, for organisms of an advanced development, a higher law than the law of personal struggle for individual existence.

Or, to proceed a step further in the direction which this criticism points out, the interests which control individual action are frequently speculative interests, while the idea of speculation is foreign to the most simple conception of society. By the word speculation is to be understood any transaction which permits a man to make a personal gain at the expense of his fellow-men. A gambler, whose earnings are balanced by the losses of those with whom he plays, belongs to the large army of speculators. The holding of real estate for a rise in value is speculation. When a merchant charges more for goods than is adequate to cover a fair return for his labor and risk in buying and arranging them for sale, he too becomes a speculator. Or should the force of competition compel him to sell goods at a loss, the speculative character of the transaction is not changed because his customers happen to be the gainers. In short, speculation consists in the endeavor to gain possession of more value than one creates, and the familiar adage that "speculation is the life of trade" shows that men have come to regard this purpose as a legitimate motive for personal conduct. But society recognizes no such interest. Society is a unity and permits of no comparative estimates. Its gains are creations of values, its losses destructions of values. How then is it possible to say that a syllogism which confounds two such diverse things as an absolute interest and a relative interest can lead to truth?

This is not exactly the manner in which Professor Cairnes presents the subject, but it is in harmony with the conclusion which he formulates. "There is no security," he says, "that the economic phenomena of society, as at present constituted, will always arrange themselves spontaneously in the way which is most for the common good. In other words, *laissez-faire* falls to the ground as a scientific doctrine." But two things are to be noticed with regard to the views of Professor Cairnes. First, he does not accept the opposing doctrine of paternal government, but holds himself at liberty to consider every question on its own merit; second, he does not appear to perceive the necessity of formulating another principle for the control of social and industrial development, which may take the place of the one whose authority he has overthrown.

> Let us be careful, (says he), not to overstep the limits of our argument. It is one thing to repudiate the scientific authority of *laissez-faire,* freedom of contract, and so forth; it is a totally different thing to set up the opposite principle of State control, the doctrine of paternal government. For my part I accept neither the one doctrine nor the other; and, as a practical rule, I hold *laissez-faire* to be incomparably the safer guide. Only let us remember that it is a *practical rule,* and not a doctrine of science; a rule in the main sound, but like most other sound practical rules, liable to numerous exceptions; above all, a rule which must never [. . .] be allowed to stand in the way of the candid consideration of any promising proposal of social or industrial reform.[14]

It is certainly granting English economy a most favorable interpretation to accept Professor Cairnes as its spokesman in this matter, and it is by no means certain that all its advocates would admit his representative character. Some economists, indeed, yet live who maintain, with heroic devotion, the philosophy of negative action, while others, who may not, perhaps, sympathize with the extreme statement of the theory of individualism, would nevertheless object to the language in which its modification is here presented. And it must be admitted that a great deal depends upon the manner in which one's views are expressed. The concessions granted by Mr. Mill, for example, amount to little when we notice how strictly he guards his exceptions to the rule, that the state should not interfere with industrial action. "*Laisser-faire,*" he says, "should be the general practice; every departure from it, unless required by some great good, is a certain evil."[15] But we need not trouble ourselves

[14] *Essays in Political Economy,* pp. 250–51.

[15] [*Principles of Political Economy,* Book V, ch. XI, sec. 7. *Editor's note.*]

with the varying views of important economists, for it will do no violence to the general trend of opinion to proceed upon the assumption that the doctrine of non-interference is now held as a maxim and not as a principle of scientific pretensions. Or to adopt the familiar phrase of those who advocate the modified form of *laissez-faire*, there is in all cases a strong presumption against state action, and in favor of what Mr. Spencer calls "the *régime* of contract."

We have now arrived at the critical point on our analysis. Is this view of the case tenable? May we rest satisfied with accepting the presumption against state activity as a sufficient guide for constructive work in economics? It will probably be conceded that this modification of the old doctrine is an advance upon the opinion which held the dogma of non-interference to be identical with the principle of individual liberty, and which assumed reasons for the latter to be arguments for the former. But the economist desires to go one step farther. The important question with him is the following: Has Professor Cairnes restored to political economy its old-time authority by admitting possible exceptions to the premise on which it is built, or has he only succeeded in marring its symmetry and destroying its logical form? It must certainly go hard with those who, educated in scientific methods, are thus left with a system of thought on their hands, from which the scientific pretension of its fundamental principle of human relations has been taken away. This amendment to the old doctrine has reduced English economy from the dignity of a science based on a principle to a philosophy based on a maxim.

And yet they who advocate the modified form of *laissez-faire* make a great parade of its authority, and urge that the old economy has not been radically changed by admitting the modification. It is to me indeed strange how a logical mind could have arrived at such a conclusion, and the only interpretation of which this seems capable is, that they who maintain it can never have fully appreciated the grand simplicity and symmetry of the old doctrines at the time when they swayed the minds of men. There was behind the Physiocrats, for example, an irresistible power when they appealed from the artificial arrangements of the eighteenth century to the authority of the law of nature. It is true there was no real thing corresponding to their conception of a law of nature, but they did not commit the strategic blunder of carrying through a line of argument on the assumption of its existence, and then proceed to classify the conditions under which society could safely disregard its demands. They did not say "there is a strong presumption" in favor of obeying nature; or that "it is a sound maxim" to obey nature; or that "it should be the general practice" to obey nature. Had they proceeded in this manner they would never have gained influence over the minds of men, for this would have been an admission that common sense is superior to a scientific principle. Yet this is the unfortunate position into which Professor Cairnes, by his trenchant analysis of the scientific claims of *laissez-faire*, has brought English economy. In its present condition it is a system of thought whose formal arguments are quite in harmony with the assumption that there exists a premise of action of scientific pretensions, but the life and force is taken from these arguments by the denial of such a premise.

The truth then, with regard to the modernized statement of English economy, as compared with its original presentation, is this: In its original form it was conclusive as an argument though based upon an erroneous premise; in its modernized form the error of its premise has been corrected, but its conclusiveness as an argument has thereby been destroyed. It is for such a reason that I cannot regard the modifications suggested by Professor Cairnes as satisfactory. I can understand Mr. Spencer, for he is logical and consistent throughout. I can even understand Professor Sumner, and take pleasure in reading his sweeping generalizations. But I cannot understand the habit of mind which rests satisfied with a philosophy of social or industrial relations not founded on principles, for such a position is wholly unscientific. It is a common complaint of men trained in the schools that practical men disdain theories. But certainly these economists of the modern English school cannot justly utter such complaint; for the practical men who deify their common sense, and who boast of judging every question on its own merits, follow to the letter the line of reasoning which the latest books lay down. English economy lost its authority because it abandoned principles and took to presumptions. It can never regain its authority until it returns to principles, though these must be broad enough and deep enough to comprehend all the various phases of activity in industrial society. This is the problem for the "new economy," and nothing but its solution can warrant the claim that a new economy has been born.[16]

My readers need not be at all solicitous lest the views here expressed should disparage the influence of the pre-

[16]I may perhaps be permitted to say in a note, though it would be out of place in the text, that I cannot regard history as adequate to take the place of the principle of individualism which has been forced to abdicate its seat of authority. History is admirable as a tool, but can never perform the functions of a principle in a system of thought. It seems to me that the problem in hand is much more difficult than many students are willing to admit. It is nothing less than the formulation of a sociology into which the science of industrial society may find its proper chapter.

sumption against the interference of the state in industrial affairs. The truth underlying the modified form of the doctrine of *laissez-faire* is unimpaired by the collapse of the elaborate argument upon which it was believed to rest. And what is that truth? Should we follow in our analysis far enough we would perceive it to be nothing but the statement of a common sense rule of conduct, viz.: that it is wise to be conservative. Any institution or custom capable of maintaining itself rightly claims presumption in its own favor as against an untried plan, however plausible. This truth, then, is the expression of the instinct of conservatism so strongly developed in the English and American character. At the present time the rule happens to hit those economists who propose to extend the functions of government, for the established thing, so far as domestic affairs at least are concerned, is individual and not governmental control. But this coincidence is an historical accident. The presumption would be against the extension of individual control if the state were in possession of the field. It is this fact, this accidental coincidence between the judgments which spring from natural conservatism and the presumption against extending the duties of the state, which deceives men, and brings them to think that the modified form of *laissez-faire* yet bears with it an authority. Its authority is nothing more than the authority which always rests with an established fact.

In the foregoing analysis I have endeavored to establish two conclusions. First, that the doctrine of *laissez-faire* cannot lay claim to scientific pretensions. Second, that the abandonment of its scientific pretension destroyed whatever authority English economy ever had as a guide for constructive expression of the instinct of conservatism. My further analysis proceeds upon the assumption that the reader is willing to grant these conclusions to have been established. It is quite natural that men who arrive at this point in their study of social relations, should turn eagerly for relief to those writers who first pointed out the error of the old system; a fact that may, perhaps, explain the readiness with which so many American economists have accepted the teachings of German investigators. The rule for separating the duties of the state from those of the individual, as laid down by German writers, is quite different from the one we have thus far considered; indeed it is the re-statement of the English rule with a reversal of its terms. In all cases of doubt, it is distinctly German to say that presumption lies with the state and against the individual. It would of course be incorrect to say that all writers hold to this rule, for, as in England there are many who are not English economists, so in Germany there are some who do not regard the state as the final thing in social analysis. But it is nevertheless true that the views just expressed are characteristic of German economic philosophy and fairly realized in German polity.

It is not my purpose to consider this rule at length. So far as it rests upon analysis it proceeds from the assumption that some industries are from their nature "sovereign in character." Thus all businesses pertaining to transportation, as railroads, expressage, telegraphy, postal service, and the like, pertain naturally to the state. These are the nerves and arteries of the body politic, and should be directed from a common center. It is indeed a little ludicrous to notice the almost superstitious reverence with which a certain class of German writers trace out the analogy existing between the social organism and physical organisms. But the more rational thought seems to be that the government may properly take the initiative and control in all forms of business which possess what is termed "the collective interest," and since so many businesses are observed to fall into this class, German writers have cut the matter short by saying that presumption lies with the state, and by throwing upon individuals the burden of proof. This contrast between the trend of the English and the German mind bears for Americans a deep significance. We have already discovered that the doctrine of *laissez-faire*, since it has passed through the hands of Professor Cairnes, amounts to nothing more than a declaration in favor of the wisdom of conservatism. We may now perceive that the rule which the German investigators adopt is also a declaration in favor of conservatism. Each people has established its practical presumption in favor of the state of affairs with which it is familiar. In England, where the philosophy of individualism permeates all thought, the presumption is in favor of private enterprise; in Germany, where the state is the center of all interests, the presumption lies in the opposite direction. Yet the mental characteristic which leads to these diverse conclusions is the same for both peoples. Is it not, then, clear that the philosophers of both schools condemn by their example any blind subservience to what they teach? And is it not absurd for American economists to array themselves in opposing schools as advocates of what is English or what is German? I am not arguing for obstinacy but for independence. The American people certainly have much that is common to both of the great peoples mentioned, but they have also much that is peculiar to themselves. Their history, though rooted in the past, is yet of their own making; their nationality is colored by the diverse sources from which their citizens are drawn; their physical surroundings have been such as to intensify a spirit of self-dependence; does it not then follow that they must build out of such material as they have at hand? Certainly no set of men should be so ready to maintain intellectual independence, in the domain of constructive economics, as they who, at the great universities of Germany, have learned how to read the true lessons from history.

It will be impossible to proceed farther without giving direct expression to my own opinions. Neither of the views respecting the relation of the state and industries which we have considered can be regarded as satisfactory, or as resting upon adequate views of the nature of society. There is no overpowering presumption in either direction, and to admit of one is to cover up the point at issue. It is true that there is a sense in which the state stands opposed to the individual, but we cannot expect to discover a guiding principle for public control so long as our analysis proceeds upon such an hypothesis. The fundamental error of English political philosophy lies in regarding the state as a necessary evil: the fundamental error of German political philosophy lies in its conception of the state as an organism complete within itself. Neither the one nor the other of these views is correct. *Society* is the organic entity about which all our reasoning should center. Both state action and the industrial activity of individuals are functions of the complete social organism. The state is not made out of the chips and blocks left over after framing industrial society, nor does industrial society serve its full purpose in furnishing a means of existence for the poor unfortunates who are thrust out of the civil or the military service. Society, as a living and growing organism, is the ultimate thing disclosed by an analysis of human relations; and because this is true it is not right to speak of a presumption in favor of individual initiative or of state control, as though these stood like contestants opposed to each other. It is not proper to consider individual activity as supplementary to state powers, or to look upon the functions of the state as supplementary to personal activity. It is futile to expect sound principles for the guidance of intricate legislation so long as we over-estimate either public or private duties; the true principle must recognize society as a unity, subject only to the laws of its own development.

PRINCIPLES THAT SHOULD CONTROL INDUSTRIAL LEGISLATION

There are two classes of thinkers with whom I have not the fullest intellectual sympathy; the one comprises those who rest satisfied with criticism, the other those whose critical analysis leads only to exhortation. Though each is useful in its way, neither renders to society the highest service of which scholarship is capable. For the end of criticism is construction, and its service should be to point out the way in which men may avoid the recurrence of mistakes disclosed. Applying this thought to the subject in hand, it now becomes our difficult task to search for those principles to which industrial legislation should conform, for there can be no greater misfortune than this, that legislation should proceed blindly, controlled only by what practical men call expediency.

Much of the confusion that now surrounds the question of the appropriate duties of government, so far as the people in this country are concerned, is due to the failure to distinguish between *laissez-faire* as a dogma and free competition as a principle. The former, as we have seen, is a rule or maxim intended for the guidance of public administration; the latter is a convenient expression for bringing to mind certain conditions of industrial society. Thus when one speaks of the benefits of free competition, one means the benefits conferred by industrial freedom. And when one argues for free competition, one is called upon to show that the best possible results may be expected for society, as a whole, and for each member of it, when labor is free and independent, when the right to acquire and enjoy property is guaranteed, when contracts are defended, and when every man is obliged to stand on his own legs, enjoying to the full the fruits of his own labor and suffering to the full the barren harvest of idleness. It seems that there should be no reasonable doubt respecting the benefits that must flow from such an organization of society, and I for one have no quarrel with those who urge its realization as a worthy object of endeavor. But I do take serious issue (and this is the important point to be observed), with those who hold that the rule of *laissez-faire* indicates the way by means of which such a state of affairs may be established and maintained. The claim that laborers should be free and independent is readily admitted, but at the same time it is denied that the language of public law, which makes all men equal before it, is a guarantee of freedom and independence; the right to acquire property is heartily endorsed, but it is also urged that property should not be acquired in such a manner, or to such a degree, as to defeat the purpose for which the right was granted; the necessity of maintaining contracts is conceded, but it must not be forgotten that the liberty of contract is a mere corollary of personal liberty. It cannot then be said that they who deny the sufficiency of the dogma of *laissez-faire* do so because they fail to appreciate the advantages of competitive action. It is true that some are open to this charge, but, on the other hand, many who believe the theory of individualism no longer applicable to modern relations, are quite willing to recognize competition as a beneficent social principle. They do, however, say that the benefits of this principle can never be realized through the uncontrolled play of private interests, carried on in harmony with existing property right.

It is unfortunate, though it is a natural consequence of the proneness in human nature to establish parties, that discussion upon this question has led to the formation of opposing schools of thought. Individualists and socialists maintain extremes of opinion respecting the nature and working of competition.[17] The former hold it to be necessarily a benevolent principle; the latter regard it as inherently a malevolent principle. Individualists, therefore,

[17]There is little need of testimony to this statement respecting individualism, but the claims of socialism may not be as familiar to my readers. I know of no better characterization of socialism as a scheme of economic thought than may be found in the six propositions upon which Louis Blanc [French socialist leader in the Revolution of 1848] based his system. I give them as summarized by Dr. Heinrich Contzen:

1. The deep and daily growing misery of the masses (*du peuple*) is the greatest misfortune.
2. The cause of the misery wherein the masses live is competition.
3. Competition is likewise for the property owners (*la bourgeoisie*) the cause of their ruin.
4. Government is the highest orderer of production and as such must be clothed with greater power.
5. The state as the greatest capitalist has this duty to perform, that through its competition private competition should be made to disappear. To this end national workshops must be established at the cost of the state.
6. Such wages must be paid as in every case to richly provide for the existence of the laborers. (*Geschichte der Socialen Frage von den ältesten Zeiten bis zur Gegenwart,* von Dr. Heinrich Contzen [Berlin, 1877], p. 128.)

would grant it the freest play, and on this account advocate *laissez-faire;* socialists would exclude it from the society which they propose to establish, at least as a directing and controlling agency, and to this end propose a socialistic state. Upon one point only do these leaders of opposing opinions agree, and that is in the opinion that the denial of one view involves the acceptance of the other. There is no peace for an economic mugwump.

Nevertheless I venture to suggest that the question here involved is not one of excluded middle. Competition is neither malevolent nor beneficent, but will work malevolence or beneficence according to the conditions under which it is permitted to act. If this very reasonable view of the case be admitted, it follows that we may escape the practical conclusions of both socialists and individualists; or at least, so far as we accept their proposals, we may rest our decisions upon some sound analysis of social relations. We may admit with Louis Blanc, that great evils follow the unbridled passion of accumulation, and recognize with Adam Smith, that personal interest in work done is the life of healthy industry; yet at the same time we may deny that the state should crush out all private control in business, and refuse assent to the doctrine that police duties exhaust the proper functions of government.

This presentation of the problem suggests the general principle according to which the relation of governmental agency to industrial affairs should be adjusted. It should be the purpose of all laws, touching matters of business, to maintain the beneficent results of competitive action while guarding society from the evil consequences of unrestrained competition. This may seem a truism, but its statement is necessary as the starting point for constructive study. It is at least sufficiently distinct from either the English or the German rule, as above stated, to warrant the belief that it may serve as the basis of a wholly different system of thought. For, according to this view of the case, neither governmental activity nor private enterprise exists by sufferance. There is no presumption for or against either the one or the other in itself considered, for both are essential to the development of a highly organized society, and the purpose of constructive thought should be to maintain them in harmonious relations.

But what are the beneficial workings of competition? Modern industrial society is built upon four legal facts: Private property in land, private property in labor, private property in capital, and the right of contract for all alike. The development of these rights, which required centuries for its accomplishment, portrays the growth of individualism and the decay of communalism and no one who fully appreciates the opportunities thus offered, as compared with the opportunities offered by an industrial society based on slavery, or on undeveloped or general proprietary rights, can seriously advocate a return to the conditions of the past. The peculiar claims urged in favor of a society organized on the competitive basis are familiar to all. Perhaps the most important of these is that men are in this manner guaranteed full enjoyment in the fruits of their labor, and on this account will be jealous in its application. Competitive society also provides for ease of movement from one grade of labor to another, or from one business to another, and thus ensures elasticity in thought and expansion of purpose as the result of the manner in which motives are applied to individual conduct. Under such conditions, it is the future and not the past that claims the attention of men.

It is hope and ambition, rather than fear and apprehension, that move the energies of men. We should not forget that the material progress of the nineteenth century is in large measure due to the mobility of action which the idea of equal rights before the law brought into modern life. It may, however, be remarked in passing that the energy displayed in modern society is due to the openness of opportunity in all forms of industry. Each competitor imagines himself the successful runner for the prize he seeks; but should the practical difficulties of attaining success ever come to be so great as to restrict the number of contestants, the healthful activity which now follows high anticipations would be replaced by the lethargy of hopelessness. It is a mistake to conclude that equal opportunities are surely maintained by granting equality before the law.

Again, wherever the conditions for competitive action are maintained, society has a guarantee that goods will be produced at the lowest possible cost; for the hope of personal gain leads to the best disposal of labor, to invention, and to the adoption of the best machinery. Assuming the same premise, society has also a guarantee that the goods produced will be placed upon the market at fair prices. It is unnecessary to enter upon any explanation of the manner in which this guarantee works, for popular economic philosophy devotes much of its attention to an elaboration of the reasoning here suggested; and our only quarrel with popular economic philosophy is that it arrests its analysis of industrial relations after discovering the advantages which might accrue to society, could the conditions for competitive action be maintained. It refuses to inquire what is necessary on the part of the state to ensure the maintenance of such conditions, or to proceed in its study to the consideration of the evils that flow from individualism in industrial life. But assuming the dogma of *laissez-faire* to be the most practical method of establishing competitive action, it shuts itself up to a sort of fatalism and witnesses with a stolid countenance the fruitless efforts of men to realize a rational existence.

But what are the evils of unrestrained competition; or, more accurately stated, what are the pernicious results of the attempted realization of competitive action under the direction of the doctrine of *laissez-faire?* I cannot hope to present a complete answer to this question, but must rest content with certain suggestions that may lead to a clear understanding of such rules for governmental action as will be proposed. The important evils of unrestrained competition are of three sorts.

First. The free play of individual interests tends to force the moral sentiment pervading any trade down to the level of that which characterizes the worst man who can maintain himself in it. So far as morals are concerned, it is the character of the worst men and not of the best men that gives color to business society.

Second. The application of the rule of non-interference renders it impossible for men to realize the benefits that arise, in certain lines of business, from organization in the form of a monopoly. The theory of *laissez-faire* sees clearly the beneficent principle in free competition, but fails wholly to recognize a beneficent principle in monopoly.

Third. The policy of restricting public powers within the narrowest possible limits tends to render government weak and inefficient, and a weak government placed in the midst of a society controlled by the commercial spirit will quickly become a corrupt government; this in its turn reacts upon commercial society by encouraging private corporations to adopt bold measures for gaining control of government machinery. Thus the doctrine of *laissez-faire* overreaches itself; for the application of the rule which it lays down will surely destroy that harmony between public and private duties essential to the best results in either domain of action.

Let us consider these suggestions in the order in which they have been presented:

THE STATE MAY DETERMINE THE PLANE OF COMPETITIVE ACTION. What is meant by saying that unguarded competition tends to lower the moral sense of a business community? This law—for I suppose in the ordinary acceptance of that term the statement here presented may be called a law of tendencies—is not of equal application to all forms of business. Wherever the personal element of a service comes prominently into view, and the character of the agent rather than the quality of goods is forced into prominence, probity has its market value and honesty may be the best policy. But in the commercial world as at present organized, where the producer and the consumer seldom come into personal contact, the moral arrangements followed in the process of production are not permitted a moment's thought. All that is considered by the purchaser is the quality and the price of the goods. Those that are cheap he will buy, those that are dear he will reject; and in this manner he encourages those methods of production that lead to cheapness.

There are of course exceptions to this rule. Some men, for example, will not wear "dollar-shirts," preferring to buy the material and see to it that living wages are paid in the making. That is, they declare a private boycott against the great establishments, because the shirts there made do not fit their consciences. An apparent exception also is found in the fact that, in almost any line of business, a few men are able to maintain themselves in the face of fierce competition by giving greater attention to the quality of goods than to the price at which they may be placed upon the market; for there is a limited number of purchasers who understand that quality is an element of cheapness. Under such conditions it is possible for the producer to incline to the leadings of his moral instincts in business affairs.

But these exceptions do not vitiate the rule laid down. There must be substantial uniformity in the methods of all producers who continue in competition with each other. Each man in the business must adopt those rules of management which lead to low prices, or he will be compelled to quit the business. And if this cheapness, the essential requisite of business success, be the result of harsh and inhuman measures, or if it lead to misrepresentation and dishonesty on the part of salesmen or manufacturers, the inevitable result must be that harshness and inhumanity will become the essential condition of success, and business men will be obliged to live a dual existence.

In his excellent work upon *The Philosophy of Wealth*, Professor Clark calls attention to the fact that the "tribal conscience," which was sensitive to the finer qualities of human character, has given way to the "inter-tribal conscience,"[18] which tolerates mercantile contention and winks

[18] [John Bates Clark (1847–1938) was at the time Professor of History and Political Science at Smith College; after serving at Amherst and Johns Hopkins, he became in 1895 Professor of Political Economy at Columbia University. In the early period his work, like that of Adams, reflected his kinship with the Christian Socialists. Clark, however, had a greater interest in the

at the tricks of trade. In making use of such expressions he probably has reference to the singular fact that, while society existed in the tribal state, or was controlled by the governments of local trading guilds, competition was inoperative so far as the members of the same tribe or city were concerned; but in case of trade between members of different tribes, or in the established market-places where citizens of various towns came together, we find the higgling of the market so characteristic of competitive transactions. At the present time, however, these local regulations have given way before the extension of the national idea, and, instead of the old mercantile code of local trade being maintained for all members of the same nation, even local trade has been brought under the direction of the rule which formerly applied only to inter-tribal commerce. Professor Clark portrays the moral effect of this transformation in the following language:

> The man of the present day is actuated now by one influence, now by the other, and has two distinct codes of outward conduct. Moral philosophy, indeed, teaches that his fundamental character is one and unchanging; but as there is one code of practical conduct for peace and another for war, so there is one code for the family, the social circle, and the church, and a different one for mercantile life. The man of business is constantly passing from the jurisdiction of one code to that of the other. . . .
>
> It is a common remark, that business practices are not what they should be, and that a sensitive conscience must be left at home when its possessor goes to the office or the shop. We helplessly deprecate this fact; we lament the forms of business depravity that come to our notice, but attack them with little confidence. We are appalled by the great fact of the moral dualism in which we live,

---

formal development of marginal theory than Adams. In this area he achieved an international reputation, especially with *The Distribution of Wealth* (1899). *Editor's note.*]

and are inclined to resign ourselves to the necessity of a twofold life.[19]

The fact upon which we insist at this point is that an isolated man is powerless to stem the tide of prevalent custom, and that in many lines of business those men whose moral sensibilities are the most blunted, exercise an influence in determining prevalent custom altogether out of proportion to their importance as industrial agents. Suppose that of ten manufacturers nine have a keen appreciation of the evils that flow from protracted labor on the part of women and children; and, were it in their power, would gladly produce cottons without destroying family life, and without setting in motion those forces that must ultimately result in race-deterioration. But the tenth man has no such apprehensions. The claims of family life, the rights of childhood, and the maintenance of social well-being are but words to him. He measures success wholly by the rate of profit and controls his business solely with a view to grand sales. If now the state stand as an unconcerned spectator, whose only duty is to put down a riot when a strike occurs (a duty which government in this country is giving up to private management), the nine men will be forced to conform to the methods adopted by the one. Their goods come into competition with his goods, and we who purchase do not inquire under what conditions they were manufactured. In this manner it is that men of the lowest character have it in their power to give the moral tone to the entire business community.

[19]J. B. Clark, *The Philosophy of Wealth* [New York, 1886], pp. 156–57. [The book was composed largely of previously published articles. Adams wrote Clark on December 10, 1886: "The articles in the *New Englander* were of great assistance to me when they appeared and I consequently look upon the book as my intellectual father born out of due season." J. B. Clark Papers, in possession of J. M. Clark. *Editor's note.*]

Mr. [William] Pitt early recognized the undue importance of the reckless and the selfish in determining the plane of competitive action. "The time will come," he said, "when manufactures will have been so long established, and the operatives not having any other business to flee to, that it will be in the power of any one man in a town to reduce the wages, and all the other manufacturers must follow." And he added, though it is not of present pertinence to our argument: "If ever it does arrive at this pitch, Parliament, if it be not then sitting, ought to be called together, and if it cannot redress your grievances, its power is at an end."[20]

The proprietor of a printing establishment in Vandewater Street remarked to me not long ago that he could point to the employers who were responsible for the harsh regulations and low wages under which the printers of the city of New York worked. "I am powerless," he added, "however much I might desire to manage my business on any other principle than that of getting the most out of the men for the least money." The business of manufacturing ready-made shirts, and in a large measure that of ready-made clothing, has fallen into the hands of disreputable men, for none others will follow the methods necessary to produce cheap goods. One of the most common complaints of business men is that they are obliged to conform to rules of conduct which they despise. It is a necessary result of a competitive society that the plane of business morals is lower than the moral character of the great majority of men who compose it.

But what, it may be asked, can the state do in the premises? The state has done much and can do more. That code of enactments known as "factory legislation" is addressed

[20]As quoted by [George] Howell in *The Conflicts of Capital and Labour* [London, 1878], p. 114.

to just this evil of competitive society, and it only remains for us to formulate for this code an economic defense. The general rule laid down for the guidance of state interference in industries was, that society should be secured in the benefits while secured against the evils of competitive action. When the large body of competitors agree respecting some given method of procedure, but are powerless to follow it because a few men engaged in the same line of business refuse to conform to the proposed regulations, it becomes the province of the state to incorporate the wish of the majority in some practical law. In this manner there is established a legal plane of competition higher than that which could be maintained in the absence of legal enactment. This is no curtailment of competitive action, but a determination of the manner in which it shall take place. If the law says that no child shall be employed in factories, the plane of competition is raised to the grade of adult labor. If married women are refused employment, the nature of competition is again changed, but competition is not restricted. Or, in the same manner, the law might establish the plane of competition to a normal day's labor for men. As the result of such legislation some of the evils of the present system would disappear, while all the benefits of individual action would yet be conserved to society.

This, then, is one defense of interference on the part of the state. It lies within its proper functions to determine the character of such competitive action as shall take place. There must be conformity of action between competitors, and the only question is whether the best or the worst men shall set the fashion. One cannot be neutral with regard to this question. No vote at all is a negative vote; and a vote in the negative is as positive in its results as one in the affirmative. Should the state insist on following the rule of non-interference, society cannot hope to adjust its productive processes to the best possible form of organization.

It may be pertinent in this connection to call attention to a thought, which, it is believed, has not received adequate attention. The opinion is frequently expressed that all the evils of modern society are traceable to the natural depravity of the individual man, and, under the direction of such an explanation, they who wish well to society expend their energies in exhorting individuals to reform their lives. This is especially the high duty of religious teachers. But have these teachers ever stopped to inquire why their persuasive eloquence has thus far met with meagre success in the reformation of society? Do they really see that, in a society where the code of business ethics conforms to the law "thou shalt love thyself better than thy neighbor," none but industrial hermits can adhere to the law "thou shalt love thy neighbor as thyself." These are certainly contradictory rules of conduct, and, so far as I am aware, no theory has ever sought to reconcile them except the one which claims that, when a man looks out for number one he looks out for his neighbor also. But our analysis has shown that the existence of such a relation is a pure assumption of optimistic natures. When Professor Cairnes demolished the scientific pretensions of *laissez-faire*, he took from us all hope of reconciling the Christian rule of ethics with the prevalent practice of Christian peoples.[21] Our religious

[21]I said above that the strength of the dogma of *laissez-faire* was the simplicity of its statement. It was also suggested in another place that the fact that it was conceived to rest upon some natural law of human relations gave it power. Another source of its influence over the minds of men is found in the fact disclosed in the text. As a philosophy of human conduct it was charmingly soothing, for, by identifying personal and social interests, it harmonized the Christian rule of conduct with the egoistic motives of business life.

teachers, whose analysis of industrial relations stops short of portraying the moral deterioration effected by unbridled competition, mean, if they mean anything, that the men whom they influence should renounce the world of business ambitions. In this fact do we find the explanation of the curious paradox, that the more effective the persuasion of religious teachers the more rapid will be the deterioration of business society; for, since the result of such persuasion must in large measure be the renunciation by men of delicate consciences of the great business opportunities, society will tend to take upon itself the moral tone of the more unscrupulous. There is great danger, while dwelling with such emphasis upon the problem of individual life, of forgetting its complement, the problem of social life.

They who recognize the pertinency of such a suggestion may find it worth their while to consider again the view of state action above presented. The state, it was claimed, can properly determine the conditions under which competition shall take place, and in this manner permit society to realize the best rather than the worst of the possible lines of actions open to it. We have all of us, doubtless, heard the claim that the state is a moral agency; that it is imposed with moral duties. For a number of years after this phrase came to my notice, it presented to my mind no distinct meaning. It seemed to me to cover the philanthropic purpose of shallow intellects, and to be most frequently used by men who knew not the way of guile nor anything else for certain. But properly understood this phrase contains a deep truth of social philosophy. It does not mean that the law is a schoolmaster coercing men to be good, nor that it is the depository of a social ideal to be admired; but on the contrary, it means that the law is an agency for the realization of the higher ideals of men by guarding them from that competition which would otherwise force them to a lower plane of action, or else force them out of business. In performing such a duty the state performs a moral function, for it regulates competition to the demands of the social conscience. Under the guiding influence of such a thought the immediate interests of the individual may be made to coincide, in some degree, with the fundamental interests of society, and thus, by disregarding the dogma of *laissez-faire,* the fundamental purpose of those formulating the doctrine is in part realized. Surely religious teachers should be interested in the opportunity which such a thought opens to men.

THE STATE MAY REALIZE FOR SOCIETY THE BENEFITS OF MONOPOLY. Let us now turn to consider the second point introduced by the enumeration of the evils that flow from unrestricted competition. The application of the rule of non-interference, it was said, rendered it impossible for society to realize for its members the benefits that arise, in certain lines of business, from organizations in the form of monopoly. It may seem at first strange to speak of a beneficent principle in connection with monopolies, for we are accustomed to associate them with all that is odious, grasping, and tyrannous. The existence of monopolies in favor of individuals has always been regarded as an infringement of personal rights, and history declares that free peoples have always revolted against the assumption of peculiar privileges by any class of men. Much of that which we have come to admire in modern life, and to rely upon in modern character, was developed in those struggles of the past to overthrow exclusive privileges, and it is on this account easy to understand the feeling of jealous distrust with which private monopolies are universally regarded. For whatever form they may assume, the results which flow from them are always in the same direction. The energies of a growing and expanding society are diverted to the service of a favored class; and this, when it becomes generally apparent, gives rise to an unhealthy discontent which checks further expansion.

But what is an industrial monopoly? An industrial monopoly may be defined as a business superior to the regulating control of competition. The peculiar privileges of the past, so far as they were of an industrial character, usually rested on royal grants or charters; but those of which complaint is now heard, spring from the conditions of modern business activity, or from the peculiar nature of certain lines of business. The distrust with which monopolies are universally regarded arises from the fact that the public is deprived of its ordinary guarantee of fair treatment, so far as it must have dealings with them. But the important thing for us to notice is, that men do not so much complain of the existence of monopolies, for they recognize the existence as inevitable, but that the peculiar privileges and unusual powers which they bestow are perverted from their high purpose to serve private ends. This fact is well illustrated in the development of the medieval craft-guilds. So long as there were no arbitrary conditions imposed for gaining membership in these guilds they were regarded with general favor; it was only after they had grown into close corporations, and when their members began to corruptly use the power entrusted to them for personal ends, that they were observed to obstruct the advance of industrial progress.

The most simple form of a monopoly is a business under the direction of a single mind, and, from the standpoint of administration, there is much to be said in favor of that harmony of control and unity of direction which such a management renders possible. Provided a business admits of something like military organization; provided the details of its management have been well worked out; provided its extension to meet new demands may be accomplished by merely duplicating what already exists; and provided the social want which it supplies is wide-spread and constant, exclusiveness in management must lead to efficiency of management, if only men of adequate ability may be found to assume authority. Under such conditions a service may be rendered at less cost to the public than if the agents of the monopoly were broken up into competing groups. There are several reasons why this is true. The fact of an assured demand for services rendered admits of the closest calculations; the extent of the demand also allows of a minute application of the principle of division of labor; the absence of any rivalry between competing concerns precludes the necessity of expending more capital than is required for an economical performance of the service; and, what is perhaps of as much importance as any other consideration, there is no temptation to adopt speculative methods of management which lead to the covering of unnecessary losses of one period by the arbitrarily high profits of another. Thus the *possibility* of cheapness and efficiency seems to lie in the very nature of a monopoly. This is the beneficent principle of which mention was made, and the practical question is how to realize the benefits of this principle for society.

The relations here set forth will present themselves more

clearly to our minds if we throw into comparison the rule of public and the rule of private financiering. A private business is managed to secure a profit, and, other things being equal, the higher the price secured for any service rendered, the higher will be the profit. The rule of private financiering, therefore, is to maintain the price of goods or services at the highest price which has no tendency to curtail profitable business. The price of goods in this case will equal the cost of production, plus the profit to the undertaker, and the only guarantee against exorbitant rates lies in the fact that purchasers are free to choose from whom they will buy.

The rule of public financiering, on the other hand, conforms to an altogether different principle. It is the purpose of government to render services at the lowest price consistent with efficient service. Price equals cost. This is true, because the state, being the manager of the business, has no motive in acquiring riches. The officers of the state receive their salaries which, roughly speaking, may be said to correspond to the profit secured by the managers of private enterprises. The guarantee that price will not be more than cost of production, including salaries of officers, lies in the publicity of accounts, and in all that goes to make up efficient service. In theory, therefore, we should expect parallel results from a monopoly under control of the state and from a business privately organized directed by the principle of free competition. For employment of corresponding grades, the salary of an official ought to be equal to the ordinary income of a business manager, and the guarantee of competition ought to work like that of official responsibility; but, unfortunately for the theory, industries vary in the demands which they make upon personal control, and neither guarantee is observed to be unrestrained in its action.[22]

I do not wish to be drawn from the main line of my argument to consider which form of organization is the most applicable to all industries; for this, I apprehend, is not the question at issue. I am arguing neither for nor against

[22]It is a significant fact for the student of social relations, that the structure of society is perfectly reflected in the classification of social studies. In France and Germany, for example, where the theory of *laissez-faire* has been less perfectly realized in internal affairs than in England and the United States, we find the science of finance pretty well differentiated from the science of political economy. This is exemplified in the existence of so clear and comprehensive a work upon finance as that of [Paul] Leroy-Beaulieu [*Traité de la science des Finances*], or in the monumental works of Wagner [*Finanzwissenschaft*] and the less pretentious treatise of [Wilhelm] Roscher [*System der Finanzwissenschaft*]. English and American writers, on the other hand, have, for the most part, followed the method of treatment laid down by Mr. Mill. He considers social relations under the name of political economy, and then, under the title "On the Influence of Government" [Book V], brings to notice a few of the questions pertaining to finance. This superficial treatment of so important a subject can only be explained by the theory of the relation of public to private duties which Mr. Mill maintained. When government is regarded as a necessary evil, and its activity as an encroachment upon the reserved rights of individuals, it is not natural that the science of finance, which treats of the material wants of the state and the means of their supply, should embrace more than a simple treatment of the theory of taxation. But among peoples who have never felt in its extreme the philosophy of individualism in industries, but who rather have sought to correlate the interests of all in the higher interests of the state, it is a necessary consequence that the science of finance should extend until it comes to be, in many particulars, the science of public administration. I have sought in the text to bring into contrast the two principles, that of private financiering which controls in political economy, and that of public financiering which controls in the administration of governmental affairs, and I have tried also to suggest that the true society can only be expected when these two complementary principles are brought into harmonious adjustment. One of the chief difficulties under which we in this country suffer, in our endeavors to solve the problem of monopolies, arises from the fact that our publicists and statesmen proceed in profound ignorance of the meaning and purpose of the science of finance. They neither understand the rules upon which public administration should proceed, nor do they perceive how a right use of the principle of public financiering may be made to serve as a check on the workings of the principle of private financiering so far as they are pernicious. Among the evidences that the doctrine of *laissez-faire* is loosening its hold upon the minds of men, will be a more extensive demand for works upon finance and administration.

state socialism. The position here assumed is, that the doctrine of *laissez-faire* does not permit society to realize in any adequate degree the benefits of organization in the form of monopoly. This is true, for several reasons, but especially because there are many industries which, from their nature, are monopolies, and cannot, therefore, be safely consigned to the guidance of the rule of private financiering. It is certainly absurd to say that a business superior to the regulating influence of competition, conducted according to the principle that the highest possible price should be demanded for services rendered, can be managed in a spirit of fairness to the public. Such a business ought to be made to conform to the rule of public financiering, but the common prejudice aroused by the teachings of *laissez-faire* renders this difficult of accomplishment. "In some countries," says Mr. Mill, "the desire of the people is for not being tyrannized over, but in others it is for an equal chance to everybody of tyrannizing."[23] I am making a use of this profound truth different from that which its author intended, when I say, that the strength of the prejudice in favor of non-interference in commercial affairs is rooted in the degrading ambition of the mercantile classes which this truth portrays. So long as public opinion holds to the presumption in favor of private management, and, as a natural consequence, refuses to enter upon a candid analysis of the nature of industries for the purpose of discovering which of them may be safely consigned to the guidance of competition, large numbers of private monopolies will be maintained. If men persist in thinking themselves free because the law grants them an equal chance with their fellow-men to become monopolists, the great

[23][*Principles of Political Economy*, Book V, ch. XI, sec. 6. *Editor's note.*]

majority will pass their lives in that state which even conservative writers call commercial dependence. Bastiat is right when he speaks of the interest of the consumer as identical with the "social interest," in so far as this question of monopolies is concerned; for it is only when we regard the problem from the point of view attained by considering the collective interest of society, that we can secure a just appreciation of the relation of government to business activity.

The practical conclusion to which this analysis leads is that society should be guaranteed against the oppression of exclusive privileges administered for personal profit, while at the same time it should be secured such advantages as flow from concentrated organization. I do not at present undertake to say whether this should be done through carefully guarded franchises, through official commissions, through competition of the state with private industries, or through direct governmental management; but in some manner this purpose should be accomplished. Such monopolies as exist should rest on law and be established in the interests of the public; a well-organized society will include no extra-legal monopolies of any sort.

But the difficulty of the rule lies in its application. Is there any principle according to which industries may be classified so that the statesman can easily determine what lines of business should be brought under the rule of public financiering? The advocates of *laissez-faire* would say that the government should wait until it was observed that society suffers some actual evil before calling into exercise the sovereign power entrusted to it. Even the most liberal of them go no farther than to admit that the presumption in favor of non-interference may be overcome by the pressure of facts. But if the view we have endeavored to present be accepted, this claim is inadequate to realize a harmonious social organization. For, in the first place, it deliberately chooses that society suffer an evil until it become unbearable before it admits of state action; and, in the second place, it incurs the risk of allowing monopolies to grow until they become stronger than the state. On the other hand, if there be any virtue in the scientific analysis of industrial relations, we should be able to determine, with some degree of accuracy, under what conditions the best results may be expected from an application of the rule of private financiering, and under what conditions the rule of public financiering will the best serve the rational ends of society, and I shall endeavor to suggest the line of thought along which such an analysis should proceed.

All industries, as it appears to me, fall into three classes, according to the relation that exists between the increment of product which results from a given increment of capital or labor.[24] These may be termed industries of constant returns, industries of diminishing returns, and industries of increasing returns. The first two classes of industries are adequately controlled by competitive action; the third class, on the other hand, requires the superior control of state power. Let us consider these a little more in detail:

Industries of the first class. Industries of the first class are such as demand a proportional increase in capital and labor to secure a given increase in product. That is to say, if $2x$ capital and labor result in $2y$ product, the application of

[24][Adams's mathematical approach was modeled on Jevons's marginal theory of capital as well as his marginal theory of exchange as found in *The Theory of Political Economy*. For Adams's high opinion of this work, see his *Outline of Lectures upon Political Economy*, 2d ed. (Ann Arbor, 1886), p. 80, and Adams's review of Jevons's *The State in Relation to Labour*, in the *Nation*, September 28, 1882. *Editor's note.*]

$3x$ capital and labor would gain $3y$ product. The increment of return is equal to the increment of capital. All those businesses in which success depends largely on attention to detail, and where the personal element of the laborer is brought prominently into view, fall under this class. For example, the retail business of merchants is subject to the rule here stated. It is not necessary for public officials to inquire if sugar is sold as low as fair dealings demand, for this business is one that admits easily of multiplication and consequently invites competition. The step from a clerkship in a grocery to the proprietorship of a new establishment is not a difficult one to take, and for this reason we are assured that the profit of an ordinary grocer will not greatly exceed the salary which he pays his head clerk. There can, therefore, be no motive for endeavoring to apply the rule of public financiering to businesses of this sort.

There are certain facts of common observation which seem to contradict the conclusion thus stated. All grocers do not secure the same income, and there are many instances of princely fortunes accumulated in trade. It is also true that of two manufacturing establishments, whose facilities for cheap production are apparently equal, the one will pay higher profits than the other. Yet such facts, properly understood, do not prove that the business in which they occur are securing monopoly prices for services rendered, but rather that they are under a management superior to the management of those industries with which they come into competition. Prices are determined by the ordinary or average cost of production, but if by superior business talent the cost of producing goods in a few establishments is less than the average, or if superior organization permits more work to be done in one establishment than in another, there is in this manner created an unusual margin between cost and price which gives rise to unusual profits. Or to state this distinction in another way: a fortune built out of a monopoly is made up from the excess of the market price over the necessary cost of production, while a fortune created by business talent springs from depressing the cost of rendering a service below the average necessary price. This distinction has not been introduced for the purpose of discussing the propriety of permitting men to enjoy the rental of their business talents, but rather to provide against a criticism sure to arise. While classifying industries according to quickness with which they respond to the influence of competition, we must not complicate our task with results traceable to the varying abilities of those who manage them. We may then repeat: Industries in which increment of product demands a corresponding increment of capital call for no regulation by law, farther than may seem necessary to determine the conditions under which competition may take place.[25]

Industries of the second class. The same conclusion applies to the second class of industries, where a given increment of product calls for a proportionally greater increment of capital and labor. Assuming the same relation to exist in an established business as before, if $2x$ capital is required for $2y$ product, an additional x of capital will not produce an additional y of product, but something less. That is to say, $3x$ capital may produce but $2\frac{3}{4}y$ product. Industries of this sort are said to be subject to the law of diminishing returns, and it calls for no abstruse argument to recognize that society is quite safe in submitting such lines of industry to the control of competition. The rate of

[25] See note 27 on page 110.

product in the new industry is greater than that in the one that is farther developed, and for this reason we may rely upon individual interest to maintain a large number of separate producers. The agricultural industry is usually cited as an illustration to which the principle of diminishing returns may be said to apply, and, if we leave out of view the element of accruing rent, the conclusion which we have suggested may be applied in its most extreme form to the business of farming. There is no call for government farming.

It is believed that the analysis, by which these two classes of industries have been disclosed, renders a service of no little importance to English economy, in that it puts a definite meaning into some of its loose expressions. We are doubtless familiar with the common argument in favor of private management. As stated by Mr. Mill, it is as follows:

> The great majority of things are worse done by the intervention of government, than the individuals most interested in the matter would do them, or cause them to be done, if left to themselves. The grounds of this truth are expressed with tolerable exactness in the popular dictum, that people understand their own business and their own interests better, and care for them more, than the government does, or can be expected to do. . . . All the facilities which a government enjoys of access to information; all the means which it possesses of remunerating, and therefore of commanding, the best available talent in the market—are not an equivalent for the one great disadvantage of an inferior interest in the result.[26]

It will be observed that this reasoning is but the emphatic expression of the truism that things are the best done when done by men personally interested in the doing; it is not,

[26]*Principles of Political Economy*, Book V, ch. XI, sec. 5. (This quotation presents a good illustration of *a priori* reasoning, for it leads to classification on the basis of exceptions to assumed premises, rather than as the result of direct analysis.)

however, satisfactory, for it is not final. Of what use is it to say that "the great majority of things" should be done by the individual, unless we can establish a clear line of exceptions to the rule laid down. It is otherwise but a maxim for the guidance of children, and a curious exemplification of a paternal philosophy. But the foregoing analysis supplies this deficiency. It puts a definite meaning into the phrase, "the great majority of things," and shows this loose classification to include such industries only as are subject to the law of constant and diminishing returns. It is true that our study regards industrial affairs from a different point of view from that of the English economists. They consider all things from the stand-point of intense production, we from the stand-point of economic distribution. But our analysis, although it has primary reference to the conditions by which the public is guaranteed against monopoly prices, serves equally well in designating those businesses in which competition will secure careful management. This conclusion follows necessarily from the fact that *the struggle for superior success in these businesses is a struggle to depress the cost of rendering services rather than to raise the prices of services rendered.*

Industries of the third class. The peculiarity of those industries belonging to the third class, which we now come to consider, lies in the fact that they conform to the law of increasing, rather than to the law of constant or decreasing returns. The increment of product from an expanding enterprise is greater than the increment of capital and labor required to secure its expansion. Adopting the algebraic formula as before, if $2x$ capital give $2y$ product, an economic application of $3x$ capital will give more than $3y$ product. Mr. Mill recognizes the relation of product to labor here pointed out, and, erroneously as it appears to me, states it as a principle of general application. "As a general rule," he says, "the expenses of a business do not increase [. . .] proportionally to the quantity of business."[27] But, without considering this point, the important thought in this connection is, that where the law of increasing returns works with any degree of intensity, the principle of free competition is powerless to exercise a healthy regulating influence. This is true, because it is easier for an established business to extend its facilities for satisfactorily meeting a new demand than for a new industry to spring into competitive existence. If this analysis of industries be accepted as correct, there can be no question as to the line which marks the duties of the state. The control of the state over industries should be co-extensive with the application of the law of increasing returns in industries.

In this matter, also, our views coincide with what seems to be the natural conclusions from the premises of English economy. Individual management is conceded to be better than state management, where success depends on the margin of profit which emerges from a careful attention to details; but, on the other hand, if success depends on the mass of business done, as must be the case in all industries subject to the law of increasing returns, the pertinency of the argument in favor of individual management loses much of its force. And more than this may be justly claimed. In-

[27][*Ibid.*, Book I, ch. IX, sec. 1.] I do not mean to say that the fact to which Mr. Mill here calls attention does not exist, but that he fails to observe its true explanation. Beyond a certain point which is quickly reached, extension in those lines of business which feel the influence of competitive action is due to superior talent for organization in him who controls it, and not to growth in demand. The margin of profit, therefore, which emerges from the curtailment of the expense account, as compared with business done, is properly chargeable to *rental* upon the business talent put into the management of the business. *Cf. ante*, p. 107.

dustries of the third class usually exist in the form of corporations, and, so far as this is true, the argument in favor of individual management is by no means conclusive in all cases. For, in the first place, the stockholders are more frequently interested in the manipulation of stock than in the management of the details of the business; and, in the second place, the responsibility and care for the detailed management of great concerns must of necessity be assigned to superintendents and agents. It does not present the true state of affairs to say that the management of a corporation will be superior to that of the government, because the men who do the work are personally interested in what they do. The accurate comparison lies between two forms of corporate management, with varying rules for appointment and election, and not between the direct control of owners and the intermediate control of agents. But let us illustrate more fully what is meant by the law of increasing returns.

The railroad business may be cited as a good illustration of this third class of industries. When a railroad is first built through a thinly settled country, it is the problem of the engineer to put the enterprise into running order at the least possible outlay of money. The survey avoids cuts and bridges even at the expense of distance; the rails are light and the rolling stock not the best. The cost of plant is necessarily great in proportion to the business that may be immediately expected. But the development of the country soon taxes the facilities of the road to its utmost, and a new road must be built, or the capacity of the old one extended through the application of fresh capital. It is not difficult to decide which of these methods will be adopted. The capacity of the old road may be extended at a cost comparatively less than would be required by the building of a new road; and, so decided are the advantages of an established business over one struggling into existence, that it is fair to regard the old road as practically free, for a long time at least, from the competitive interference of new capital.

It may be regarded as a little rash to bring up, by way of illustration, an industry about which there is so much discussion. Many writers, who look at the question rather as railroad lawyers than as students of social organization, maintain that the business of inland transportation is subject to the regulative influence of competitive action and this they endeavor to prove by calling attention to the fall in through freights. Mr. Edward Atkinson,[28] for example, seems to think the last word on the subject to have been said when he calls attention to the fact that a laborer in the city of New York can afford to eat bread from wheat grown in Dakota.[29]

Out of deference to my readers, however, I will pass this discussion with the suggestion that it is an error to judge of the efficacy of competition in the railroad industry, solely on the basis of freight schedules. There are other tests equally as clear and much more simple in their application. In any business subject to competition, a new enterprise of the same sort as one already established, and bidding for the same trade, ought to spring up in the ordinary course of industrial expansion, and not be delayed until the hope of enormous speculative profits shall induce to such an undertaking. Or, to state the point specifically, if it be true that

[28] [Atkinson, *The Distribution of Products* (New York, 1885), pp. 286–87. Atkinson was an outstanding, wealthy Boston journalist-economist, and a prominent figure in insurance and textile circles. For a valuable biographical study, see H. F. Williamson, *Edward Atkinson* (Boston, 1934). *Editor's note.*]

[29] [Dakota referred to the Dakota Territory which comprised what are now the states of North Dakota and South Dakota and the eastern parts of Wyoming and Montana. *Editor's note.*]

competition rules in the railroad business, the chief purpose of building new lines within the territory of an established line, should not be to make money by selling out to the stockholders of the line already doing the business. There can be no money in such a speculation unless the net receipts of the old road are far in excess of the normal return upon the necessary cost of its plant. For, as has been pointed out, were it the increased traffic which suggested the necessity of increased facilities, these could be more economically supplied by extending the capacity of the established line. It is because certain corporations are gorged with profit that they may be successfully bled by competing concerns of mushroom growth; and it thus appears that the very fact so frequently cited by corporation lawyers as proof of the efficacy of competition is evidence of the inability of this principle to secure fair dealings to the public.

Or again, our comparison of the rule of public and of private financiering leads to the conclusion that, when the guarantees upon which each respectively rests are unimpeded, parallel results may be expected in all forms of industry. From this it follows that personal income from personal services should be about the same for all businesses of the same grade. But compare the salaries of public officials with railroad officials; or the salaries of railroad officials who are "let in on the ground floor," with those of employés whose duties are quite as important for the proper management of the business, but of a more perfunctory character. Or consider the salaries that men pay themselves for rendering that service so important to society of manipulating stock; or again, the large amounts gotten out of the earnings of the roads in the form of lawyers' fees, arbitrators' fees and the like, before any dividends are declared.

Profit is what a man pays to himself when he employs himself, and where competition works its normal results no man can pay to himself very much more than he will be obliged to pay to other men for services of the same grade. I will not call this excess of self-payment evidence of corruption, as would be done if a man were in the employ of the government, for the law has nothing to urge against it; I only say that competition does not regulate those businesses where great discrepancies of personal income are permanently maintained among men of equal talent.

There are many other lines of business which conform to the principle of increasing returns, and for that reason come under the rule of centralized control. Such businesses are by nature monopolies. We certainly deceive ourselves in believing that competition can secure for the public fair treatment in such cases, or that laws compelling competition can ever be enforced. If it is for the interest of men to combine no law can make them compete. For all industries, therefore, which conform to the principle of increasing returns, the only question at issue is, whether society shall support an irresponsible, extra-legal monopoly, or a monopoly established by law and managed in the interest of the public. In this latter way may the benefits of organization in the form of monopoly be secured to the people, and in no other. The great argument against public monopolies is that government is inefficient and corrupt, and this brings us to a consideration of the third class of the evils which result from the theory of non-interference as maintained in modern society.

SOCIAL HARMONY MAY BE RESTORED BY EXTENDING THE DUTIES OF THE STATE. As the third class of evils attending the attempted realization of the doctrine of *laissez-faire*, may be mentioned the injury worked to establish government. The policy of restricting public powers within the narrowest possible limit tends to weaken government and render it inefficient; this leads to corruption on the part of public officials, which, in its turn, invites to yet greater corruption in private practices. Excluding for the present Federal administration, no one will deny the inefficiency of the government of our states, while that of our municipalities is generally regarded as a dead failure. This fact is urged by the advocates of *laissez-faire* as the strongest argument in favor of their doctrine. See, they say, what a weak and halting thing this government is; it cannot do well what now is in its hands, how absurd to extend the range of its activity! There seems to be sound sense in this statement; and yet, notwithstanding its apparent reasonableness, it is believed to rest upon superficial reasoning, for it commits the grave error of mistaking a result for a cause. I would not go so far as to say that the statement would be wholly true if turned end for end, but there is truth in the charge that the inefficiency of local government is in large measure traceable to the endeavor to realize the *noli tangere* policy among a people whose energies are directed by the commercial spirit.

The advocates of non-interference have treated government as the old physicians were accustomed to treat their patients. Was a man hot he was bled; was he cold he was bled; was he faint he was bled; was he flushed he was bled; until fortunately for him he passed beyond the reach of leech and lance. This has been, figuratively speaking, the form of treatment adopted by the people of the United States for their local governments, and it has worked its natural result of feebleness and disintegration.

It is quite possible that some of my readers will protest against such a presentation of the case, resting their criticism upon the well-known tendency towards an increase in legislation in these latter days. This is what Mr. Spencer complains of, and it is also the occasion of that remark, so often heard, that sessions of legislatures are far too frequent. But there are two thoughts which suggest themselves in reply to such a criticism.

Firstly. The multiplication of laws, so far from being out of harmony with the theory of individualism as understood by democratic peoples, is a natural consequence of its general acceptance. A philosophy of social relations, like that of *laissez-faire*, which tends to efface the sharp distinction between public and private interests, must inevitably result in an extension of pernicious legislation; for, under the direction of such a philosophy, men feel themselves warranted in using public machinery for private ends. This conclusion is fully sustained by considering the nature of the bills which gain the approval of our modern law-making bodies. The larger number of these are bills urged and passed for private ends. It is not claimed that such a result is chargeable to corruption, (a moderate amount of which must always be allowed for in reasoning upon public affairs), nor does it necessarily show that the interests of the public are consciously overlooked by their appointed guardians; but this fact is believed to be tenable evidence that the premises of individualism have gained so firm a hold upon the common mind that legislators are prone to identify the interests of the public with those of individuals.

Secondly. It is believed that the above criticism mistakes the true center of public power. The importance of government, or the extent of the functions assigned to it, is not measured by the amount of legislation which its law-making bodies turn off from year to year, but rather by the nature of the administrative duties imposed upon it, or by the extent of the powers assigned to its courts. Indeed, the stronger the executive and judicial departments of a government, the less opportunity will there be for particular legislation, and the more likely will it be that such laws as are passed will conform to the just requirements of general laws. It is especially the administrative functions of government that the doctrine of *laissez-faire* attacks; and the strength of the attack lies in this, that individuals desire the opportunity of performing services of "collective interest" under the ordinary rule for private financiering. It must, then, be admitted that the above criticism does not touch the point. The increased legislation which we all deplore does not prove that *government* is growing strong and extending its range of duties; it is rather the evidence of increasing weakness, for it shows that government is incapable of adequately defending the public against the encroachment of individuals.

The constitutional history of the various states of the Union, so far as it pertains to the legal restrictions imposed upon their administrative powers, bears directly upon the point under consideration. I cannot, of course, present even the outline of this history, but there are two facts well worth a moment's notice. The contemporaneous growth of the power of corporations, on the one hand, and of municipal corruption, on the other, bears for us a deep significance. The rise of corporations into such power that they menace the stability of society, by controlling in their favor legislation, dates from the time when the states were deprived of all direct control over inland transportation. It will be remembered that between the years of 1830 and 1845 it was the accepted policy in this country for the states to undertake the building of railroads and canals. The Board of Internal Improvements was a familiar figure in local politics, and the business intrusted to it was as important as any that claimed public attention. For quite a number of reasons which might be mentioned this industrial experiment of the states ended disastrously, and left the local governments involved in debt; and it was the reaction in public sentiment occasioned by the taxes imposed to meet public obligations which led the people to so amend the constitutions that the states could never again undertake industrial duties.

The states being thus forced into the background, the way was left clear for the development of private enterprise and corporate management. But it was a mistake to suppose that private capital was adequate to meet the needs of a growing country. The two hundred and fifteen millions of acres of public lands granted by the Federal government to these corporations; the one hundred and eighty-five millions of municipal bonds issued for the building of railroads; the many instances of local taxes paid to construction companies; all testify to the inadequacy of the theory adopted. It is no occasion for surprise that legislation for private ends greatly increased.

But the spirit thus engendered did not rest satisfied with placing restriction upon the industrial powers of the states, in order to make room for private enterprise in the building of railroads and canals. In all matters where any possible question arose between government and corporations, the advocates of governmental control were obliged to prove their case. At the present time the water-works in many of our towns are managed by private companies. It is the exception for gas to be supplied through public works, while there is no city, so far as I am aware, that maintains control over its street railways. And in perfect harmony with this whole line of policy is the morselization of government among separate and independent boards, rather than the concentration of power in the hands of responsible officials in such a manner as to make it worth their while to attend to business. Under the sway of this policy, municipal government has become corrupt, while in many cases corporations have passed the bounds of all decency. These two tendencies have developed contemporaneously, and the question is whether there is any causal relation between them.

As I view the matter, there is certainly a close connection between the rise of the menacing power of corporations and the rise of municipal corruption. They are both an inevitable result of the too great confidence that has been placed in the regulative potency of competition, on the one hand, and of the too great suspicion with which governmental action is viewed, on the other. It is impossible, as society is at present organized, properly to correlate public and private duties. The motives leading men in one direction are overpoweringly strong when compared with the motives leading in the other direction. And, under such circumstances, it is futile to expect that either domain of activity will exercise a healthful regulating influence upon the other.

The basis of this distinction has been already suggested.[30] We have said that society, being the fundamental fact dis-

[30]It may be right to say that, for a few pages following, this essay quotes from a somewhat comprehensive study upon Public Debts, about to appear from the press of Messrs. Appleton & Co., of New York City [*Public Debts*, (New York, 1887), pp. 367–75]. My apology for thus making double use of the same manuscript is, that the address of which this monograph is an expansion was not intended for wide circulation; but, having attracted some attention in its original form, it seems a little pedantic to now change the wording, merely to avoid formal repetition.

closed by an analysis of human relations, confines within itself all individual growth and action. The activity which it displays is either public or private; that is to say, the activity of the state embracing all governmental functions, or that of individuals or corporations which is undertaken for private ends. But the important point that should be noticed in this connection is, that these departments of social activity are constantly acting and reacting each upon the other. The line which separates them is clearly defined so far as the principles are concerned to which each must conform, for the one is subject to the rule of public and the other to the rule of private financiering; but the growth of society demands continuous modification in the assignment of specific functions. Recognizing then the mutual relations that exist between public and private duties, it is easy to understand why failure to achieve the best results in one department of activity must injuriously affect the other; and the pertinent question for one who would direct by his thought the development of society is, under what conditions may the best results be expected from both departments of activity?

This question has already been answered. The best results may be expected when the duties assigned to public officials, and the functions performed by private individuals, are so correlated that the inducements offered are of about the same strength in both domains of activity. It is of course necessary, in applying this rule, to take in consideration other than merely pecuniary motives by which men are led to act. Considerations of social distinction, the desire to exercise such powers as one may possess, the pleasure of filling well a responsible position, indeed all the varied demands of human nature must be admitted into the account. If the importance of the state is so emphasized, and the allurements in the form of social position or emoluments of office are so strong, that the best talent of the people is drawn into the public service, a powerful and efficient government will probably be established, but a very bad society. It is believed that Prussia is now suffering from the dearth of talent and vigor in common business enterprises, and that she must continue to suffer in this manner until the state relaxes its hold upon the brilliant and talented of her youth. A German sewing machine is a very bungling affair, made after the abandoned models of American patterns; but German cities are well governed.

In our own country, on the other hand, one observes that society has developed in the opposite direction. The great prizes here offered are in the line of individual initiative. Our civil service is so poor that an official has no social position, while a business man who accumulates money is generally regarded with deference. The salary paid by the state is nothing when compared with what men of ordinary talent may secure, either as profit if engaged in business on their own account, or as salary if working for a private employer. It is, therefore, no occasion for surprise to learn that in this country we have very perfect sewing machines, but poorly administered cities.

One cannot fully appreciate this view of the case without calling to mind the possibilities of acquiring wealth in a rapidly developing industrial society. The atmosphere of such a society is intensely commercial, and not only do men of ability and energy refuse to consider a public position as desirable for themselves, but they regard with supercilious condescension one who is willing to assume public office in a municipality. And it may be added in this connection, as bearing on the question of municipal corruption, that the moral judgments of a public officer are very much like those of his neighbors who elect him, and the sentiments which control in the transaction of their daily business will probably give color to his administration. But the ordinary business life of the nineteenth century is such as to render men familiar with methods of speculation, and to conform their ethical principles to the law of supply and demand. The spirit of speculation partakes in character of the spirit of gambling. It judges all businesses undertaken on the basis of their pecuniary success, and has little care for the equivalent given for what is gained. A fine sense of what is just cannot exist where it prevails, nor can a delicate appreciation of what is honest be long retained by business men.

Suppose now, that a man of good intentions come into office in a community breathing the atmosphere of commercial speculation (let us say the office of Mayor in his town or Governor in his state), what does he see upon looking into the society whose welfare is placed in his hands? He sees it to be no uncommon thing, where contracts are uncontrolled, and where the rule of individual ownership is indiscriminately applied to all of the agencies of production, that fortunes are established in the hands of men and families having no peculiar right to them. Men who are lucky in owning real estate that other men want; men whose mines happen to yield purer copper than other mines worked; men with timber lands, salt wells, and other gratuitous products of nature that come into demand as population increases; all these increase their pecuniary importance out of proportion to their effectiveness as producers of wealth. He sees also, that many businesses which, from their very nature, must be carried on as monopolies, are given over to private control, that the principle of private financiering is applied to them with all its vigor, and that in this manner large fortunes are accumulated and large power over men acquired, exceeding by far the importance of any individual to society. He sees also that in many businesses, naturally subject to the regulating influence of competition, artificial combinations are established by means of which monopoly prices are secured from consumers. But such privileges as these cannot pass unchallenged, and it follows that the important lawyers of every town are retained at large salaries to defend by their tempered talents the privileges that monopolists have secured; while other lawyers are hired to depart from their legitimate profession to secure for business men some special legislation. Yet all this lies within the law. It cannot be branded as corrupt, although the least sum taken by a public official beyond his stated salary is properly called robbery.

As contrasted with this state of affairs, what does our successful candidate see in the office to which he has been elected? He will not long remain an incumbent before discovering that the position which he sought as a dignity brings with it no honor. What he thought to be a place of responsibility and power proves to be the center of no great influence, demanding in reality little beyond the perfunctory duties of a ministerial officer. He finds that there is small demand for the exercise of judgment and narrow play for the development of manly faculties;[31] he also learns, through the sinister suggestions of those whose personal interests he does not forward, that his tenure of office is in-

[31] A tendency towards municipal reform has lately shown itself, which will in some degree set aside such criticisms as those expressed in the text. I refer to the abolition of special boards and the concentration of responsible power in the hands of the mayor. And yet it cannot be admitted that such a change in the mechanism of government can reach the seat of the evil. Municipal corruption is merely one of the symptoms of social disorder.

secure; and, last of all, he finds that his salary does not suffice to keep his family respectably in the social circles in which they wish to move, and that the gratitude of republics does not extend to provision for their servants against sickness and old age. Repeating again the assumption that our candidate is honest, at least within the meaning of the law, and that he is conscious of ordinary business capacity, we are warranted in concluding that the career of an official will not harmonize with his tastes. He will, upon the first opportunity, retire to private life, which presents larger scope for efficient activity, and where the prizes to be gained are much greater.

Such are the conditions of a public career in most of the municipalities of the United States, and the observed results are altogether what might have been expected. The incumbents of local office are usually men of indifferent ability. If not actually depraved, they are at least colorless in character. Among "city fathers" of this sort there appears, from time to time, the shrewd yet unscrupulous man who, for personal aggrandizement, assumes complete control over public affairs. This is the explanation of "rings" and "jobs." Public corruption, therefore, is no accident. It is the necessary result of the idea that the best thing to do with a public official is to lay him on the shelf out of harm's way.

Is it not, then, correct to say that the theory of noninterference, which regards individual enterprise as the only proper depository of industrial power, and which relies wholly on competitive action as the guarantee of fair treatment in business affairs, is an obstacle to the restoration of harmony in social relations? Under the influence of the sentiment engendered by this theory, we see corporations to have attained power at the expense of the importance of the states;

we see the symmetry of government to have been destroyed by the unwarranted extension of its legislative functions; we see the line between public and private interests to have been practically effaced by the prevalent philosophy of formal optimism, and, as a natural consequence, the machinery of government easily perverted from its high purpose to serve the private ends of corporations and individuals; and, what is worse than all else, we are beginning to see these disintegrating and enfeebling tendencies to bear their normal fruitage of political corruption and governmental incompetency. I am not arguing for any particular line of public policy, but rather for a change in the attitude of mind with which men commonly regard the agency of government; for great reforms are, after all is said, nothing but a change in the way people look at things.

THE TEST OF CONSERVATISM

No one can be more conscious than myself of the incompleteness of the foregoing analysis, nor of the danger incurred that so hasty a presentation may give rise to conclusions for which I would not wish to be held responsible. And it may not be inappropriate to say, as guarding somewhat against misunderstanding, that I consider the attitude of mind by which this essay has been directed to be essentially conservative. It stands opposed to anarchy on the one hand, which is individualism gone to seed; and to socialism on the other, which, both historically and logically, is a revolt against the superficial claims and pernicious consequences of *laissez-faire*. Its purpose is to conserve true democracy, and this it would do by weakening the influence of commercial democracy which now rules the minds of men.

That my readers may see more clearly what is meant by a conservative application of the principles which our analysis has disclosed, I venture to suggest the lines along which further study might with profit be pushed. The social problems of the present day, so far as they are forced upon us by the prevailing tendencies of industrial affairs, are of three distinct classes. The first may be termed the question of constitutional development; the second the question of monopolies; the third the question of labor-relations. All of these questions are intimately connected, and should be solved with a view to the mutual interests which they represent.

But before speaking directly of these problems, let us call attention to the critical point at which the people of this country have arrived in the process of their development as a nation. Other countries have the apparent advantage of being made up of homogeneous peoples, and, to a certain extent, of having to do with problems which spring from the unfolding of homogeneous ideas. This is not the case in the United States. The citizens of this country come from various parts of the world, bearing with them their race-thoughts and hereditary inclinations; and it thus comes about that, upon American soil, the conflicting ideas of older peoples have found a battle-ground. This, says the confirmed optimist, must lead to the establishment of a strong civilization, for only the best traits of the mingling races will be conserved. This, says the confirmed pessimist, will certainly prove the destruction of whatever by accident is good in American institutions. For myself, professing to be neither a fatalist optimist nor a fatalist pessimist, but professing rather to recognize the social destiny of man to lie largely under his own control, this mingling of races and of diverse ideas serves only to impress strongly upon my mind that the present is a critical epoch in the history of the American people.

But what are the ideas contending for mastery? What are the alternatives between which the people of this country are called upon to choose? Without specifying too minutely, we may say that most of the problems now claiming attention may be solved either by a further application of the principle which characterizes English political philosophy, or by an adjustment of our social relations to the principle which underlies German polity. The former lays stress upon the importance of the individual, and endeavors to define his rights by holding those who exercise power to a strict account. The latter looks in the opposite direction. It would merge the personality of the individual into that of the state, believing his rights to be guaranteed by massing so much power in the hands of the government that no motive can exist for administering public affairs in a tyrannous manner. That is to say, to speak in language more common, though perhaps no more easily understood, the American people are obliged to choose between the principle of individualism and the principle of socialism.

It is a mistake to admit of any compromise between these ideas. We might as well suggest to a traveler that he had better compromise between going east or going west in search of sunshine, and advise him to take his way northward.[32] The suggestion that the society of the future will be

[32]Mr. [Henry] Hyndman has committed an historical blunder in the very title which appears upon the cover of his book [*Historical Basis of Socialism in England* (London, 1883)]. There is no "Historical Basis of Socialism in England." What Mr. Hyndman has shown is, that the theory of industrial rights in England has not kept pace in its development with the theory of political rights, and that an industrial mechanism has grown up which has not proven equally beneficial to all classes of Englishmen. But such a

the survival of whatever is best in both socialism and individualism is evidence to my mind of a lack of intellectual discernment, for it springs from the pernicious habit of classifying social movements according to their external form, rather than by the life-giving principle which underlies them. Is public support of education socialistic or individualistic? Is the ownership of gas works by the municipal corporation socialistic or individualistic? My reply is, you cannot tell until you are acquainted with the consensus of opinion which permits these duties to be brought under the control of government. Socialism is more than a form of society, though neither its advocates nor its critics appear to appreciate the fact.

Were it my purpose to develop the line of thought thus suggested in a logical manner, it would be necessary at this point to show why the American people should hold to the English theory of personal liberty rather than adopt the German theory of state supremacy; but such an undertaking would carry me far beyond the appropriate limits of a monograph. Indeed, my only further purpose is to show what is meant by the claim that the relation of government to industrial action, portrayed in this essay, is of essentially a conservative character; and this can be done in no clearer manner than by calling attention to the fact that the views entertained are the natural and necessary development of that principle of political liberty fundamental in English political philosophy. The opinions expressed in this essay

---

portrayal does not disclose an historical basis for socialism, for the development of which he speaks has not changed the quality of thought which gives character to the average Englishman. The sense of personality is stronger now than ever before. There can be no historical basis of socialism in England until the historical forces have changed the character of Englishmen. [Hyndman was a wealthy, avowed follower of Marx.]

are motived by the theory of individualism, and not by the theory of socialism. They trace the evils of existing society to the fact that the principle of personal responsibility in the exercise of social powers has been arrested in its development, and they look for escape from present difficulties to the extension of this principle in industrial affairs. It is inaccurate to regard such a position as a compromise with socialism, or as an abandonment of the true spirit of English economic philosophy, or as a "reaction in political economy." It is true that the theory of governmental action, for which this essay contends, would press the principle of personal responsibility farther than it has yet been applied; but it is nevertheless conservative, for its aim is to bring industrial society into harmony with the fundamental thought of our political constitution. There is no other escape from socialism.

But how does the theory of industrial responsibility fit into the social problems? The first service which it renders is to limit the claims of any particular question. It draws, for example, a clear line between the labor question and the monopoly question. The nature of the responsibility in the first instance pertains to the relations which an employer, as the administrator of industrial power, holds to the men whom he employs; the nature of the responsibility in the second instance holds the employer and his men, together representing an industrial organization, accountable for the manner in which they serve the public. Nothing can lead to greater calamity than the confusion of these two questions, for the method of treatment is essentially different for each. The labor question has to do with the internal organization of particular industries; it contemplates labor relations, and holds in view the rights and conditions under which work is done. All the matters which it considers must be adjusted on the basis of free contracts; for to settle them in any other way would result in the destruction of legal liberty. It is sometimes urged as against this conclusion that the Justices of the Peace in old England could fix wages; this is true, but it should be remembered that they could also order a man to be flogged who would not work at the wages fixed. It follows, then, that the labor question is not, and from its nature can never become, a political question, and they deceive themselves who suppose a well-crystallized political party may be erected upon the interest which it represents. And it should be noticed that the rules of interference of government with industrial action, which have been stated above, do not contemplate the solution of the labor problem. Indirectly, it is true, the state may lend its influence in such a solution by enacting laws for raising the plane of competitive action. Possibly, also, boards of legal arbitration may be established with some degree of success for some particular industries; but such measures do not touch the vital point of the labor controversy.

With the monopoly question, on the other hand, the state has everything to do. This is of necessity a political question; and, while it may be true that the laboring class is more directly interested in it than other classes, it is yet a question which touches the interests of all who are consumers of goods. And it is most unfortunate that the leaders of the workingmen in this country have so confused the labor question with the monopoly question, that even men of considerable discernment believe them to be identical; for this confusion leads the conservative public to oppose every change in industrial affairs, thinking all changes to be necessarily in the direction of socialism. But one who appreciates the theory of personal responsibility cannot be thus deceived. There is a natural and an eternal enmity between the principle which underlies the conception of English liberty and monopolies of every sort, whether they be individualistic or socialistic. It is an intellectual blunder to say that all extensions of the functions of government are in the direction of socialism, for it may be that such a movement contemplates merely the extension of responsible control over a business which would be otherwise irresponsibly managed. Such an extension of governmental duties, therefore, finds its warrant in English political philosophy. The occasion for complaint is oppression, and not a particular form of oppression. A tyranny which springs from the unregulated workings of self-interest is as pernicious in its results, and presses as hardly upon the individual, as a tyranny which rests upon political privilege. And, if this essay have any merit, it consists in its candid recognition that the science of industrial society has not rendered to humanity the highest service of which it is capable, until its analysis of social relations discovers some principle for the guidance of legislation in directing or limiting competitive action. It was to this end that industries were classified as subject to the law of constant, increasing or diminishing returns; for it is on the basis of some such classification that legislation must proceed in dealing with the question of monopolies.

The third question in the social problem, as above portrayed, pertains to the proper residence of political power for the control of industrial action. This is indeed a broad question. A glance at the structure of government in the United States shows it to be adjusted to the requirements of two leading ideas: the one pertaining to the balance of authority between the various departments which together make up government; the other to the balance of authority between the various grades of government which together make up the nation. It is this latter characteristic which is of importance to the present discussion. The theory of democracy, in addition to urging that power should only be placed in the hands of responsible agents, demands that all powers granted should lie as closely as possible to those upon whom they are exercised. This is equivalent to saying that local governments are the stronghold of democracy, and that they who profess to believe in democracy should come to the defense of the states against encroachments upon their original powers. It need hardly be said that the states have lost their importance as administrative centers. The encroachments of congressional action, on the one hand, and of the private corporations on the other, have reduced them to relative incompetency, and they are not now regarded as capable of dealing with such questions as the development of industrial society would naturally impose upon them. So far as the Federal government is concerned, the extension of its powers thus far does not seem to be open to severe criticism, and we are only solicitous as to what this tendency will bring about in the future. The present condition of affairs is easily stated. Men are now coming to realize the disastrous consequences likely to emerge from the continued sway of irresponsible corporate power. They see that an extension of governmental agency can alone retain for them the fruits of an advanced industrial civilization; and, inasmuch as the states are incompetent to deal with such difficult questions, they turn of necessity to the Federal government. There is, of course, room for honest difference of opinion as to the desirability of such a tendency, but the fundamental point at issue should not be obscured in the hasty agitation for relief from pressing evils. It should be held firmly in mind that they who advocate the extension of Federal powers do not seek to conserve the American theory of government. They are Imperialists, and not Federalists.

This essay may then be regarded as a plea for the old principle of personal responsibility as adequate to the solution of all social, political and industrial questions; but it is at the same time urged that this principle must be accepted fearlessly and applied without reserve. It has not been attempted to portray the nature of this responsibility as regards labor relations; for this essay was limited to a consideration of the proper industrial functions of the state, and it is believed that the labor problem must be worked out on the basis of freedom of contract. To admit that the state should control labor relations is to admit the essential point in socialism. But the attitude of this monograph is different with regard to monopolies. These, it is claimed, should be controlled by state authority, and it is suggested that the American theory of political liberty will lead men to rely as far as possible upon the efficiency of local governments in the exercise of such authority. When one considers the present attitude of private corporations towards the public, and the relation which exists between the Federal government and the state governments, he is constrained to say that the times are ripe for the rise of a democratic party.

Economics and Jurisprudence

Presidential Address before the American Economic Association

It is with no thought of subjecting to analysis any abstruse doctrine of political economy, or of discussing any legal question as a lawyer might discuss it, that I invite your attention for the few moments I have the honor to address you, to a consideration of the relation between Economics and Jurisprudence. My purpose, though less comprehensive, is more definite. Convinced as I am that much of the confusion in economic theory and much of the discord in industrial life, are alike due to inadequate expression by formal law of fundamental industrial rights, I desire to point out, as well as I may, the character of that confusion and discord, and to suggest the line along which evolution in jurisprudence must proceed in order that harmony in economic theory and peace in the business world may be established.

It may be well at the outset to explain the cast of meaning attached to the word jurisprudence. As employed throughout this discussion it does not seek to confine the mind to the idea of positive law; that is to say, to statutory enactments or court precedent. From Cicero we learn that "the study of law must be derived from the depths of philosophy, and by an examination of the human mind and human society principles may be discovered in comparison with which the rules of positive law are by trivial importance." It is in this larger sense that use is made of the word jurisprudence. The idea which it conveys strikes at the root of human relations, and the reasoning which it implies touches rights and duties that are fundamental. It is at once a philosophy, a science, and an art. As a philosophy, its desire is to understand justice; as a science, its purpose is to explain the evolution of justice; as an art, its aim is to formulate those rules of conduct essential to the realization of justice. Conceived in this manner, jurisprudence forms the background of all associated activity; it provides the framework that limits and controls the exercise of liberty; it reflects the color and resounds the tone of those unconscious premises of action which give character to a civilization. The law is neither a schoolmaster for instruction, nor a guardian for command; it is, rather the expression of the ethical sense of a community crystallized about the problem of common living.

Now, it is clear that jurisprudence, defined as I have endeavored to define it, must be subject to a development corresponding to that of a society whose ethical ideals it is designed to express. It may be true that justice as a philosophic concept is the same for all peoples and at all times, but whether this be true or not, the rules for the guidance of conduct vary with the ever varying conditions under which that conduct takes place. Thus, every change in the social structure, every modification of the principle of political or industrial association, as well as the acceptance of a new social ideal, must be accompanied by a corresponding change in those rights and duties acknowledged and enforced by law. Should this development in jurisprudence be arrested or proceed sluggishly, as compared with that of some particular phase of associated action, serious mischief will inevitably follow. This is true because such unequal development would evidence the general appreciation by men that the law fails to express rights which they hold to be fundamental; and it is the universal testimony of history that every desire for a right or a privilege common to any considerable number of men, yet of such a sort that it is opposed by the common law of conduct, will find expression through an appeal to a higher law, a divine law, a natural law, an ethical claim, an historic necessity, or some other phrase pressed into the service of agitators whenever an appeal is taken from that which is to that which should be. If, now, this desire, asserted as a natural right merely because it is not acknowledged by the philosophy of jurisprudence, be in reality an historic product, and, therefore, an enduring force, it is futile to expect the restoration of harmony until either the established system of jurisprudence shall assert its authority and repress the aspiration of those who seek the orderly expression of unusual rights, or until, this aspiration being acknowledged as just, the interest which it represents is incorporated in a reformed system of jurisprudence. In the one case, harmony of life will be restored but progress arrested; in the other, harmony will be realized as the result of progress.

In all this there is nothing new. This theory respecting the evolution of approved conduct is found in all treatises upon the Science of Jurisprudence. The sense of a right, must, from the nature of the case, precede the expression of a right. The stimulus of moral fervor is essential to a reform in the social order. The only strange thing in the situation is that, while this is easily seen with regard to controversies of the past, it is with difficulty appreciated when a controversy that touches our lives is the subject of analysis; and what I have to say this evening, will interest you, not because it contains any novel conception respecting the evolution of jurisprudence, or the content of economics, but rather because it is an effort to consider the present industrial situation in the light of this acknowledged evolutionary process, and to derive from this consideration some help in answering the many perplexing questions of ethics and expediency that arise from out the social turmoil in which we live.

So broad a theme cannot, of course, be adequately presented in a single address, and my further remarks will, therefore, be confined to the elucidation of three points designed to show how the industrial development of the past one hundred years has disturbed the once harmonious relations between economics and jurisprudence. I shall, in the first place, endeavor to explain why the individualism of the eighteenth century fails to express the moral necessities of the present industrial order. I shall, in the second place, endeavor to show that the principle of responsibility, which is the cornerstone of English jurisprudence, is incapable of industrial application under existing industrial conditions. I shall, in the third place, consider what is necessary for the realization of industrial liberty and attempt to place in its proper light the assertion that there is no industrial liberty without industrial property.

I

Following the order suggested, our first task is to explain how the industrial development of the past one hundred years, starting under the protection of an industrial philosophy approved by the advanced thought of the time, has wrought such changes in the organization and structure of industry, that the philosophy in question is now regarded as a retained advocate for the conservative interests of society. We need not pause to describe this philosophy.

The individualism of the eighteenth century is something very real in the world of thought, and its application to industry suggests the content of English political economy. The spirit of this philosophy is found in Adam Smith when he protests in the name of natural law against positive law and established customs; it is found in [David] Ricardo when he accepts the margin of profit as the measure of potential progress; it is found in [Nassau] Senior[1] when he applies his doctrine of saving to the solution of all industrial problems he sees fit to recognize; it is found in John Stuart Mill, and is the explanation of his attempt to crystallize industrial analysis about the commercial law of supply and demand. Speaking generally, industrial expression is given to this philosophy in the doctrine of *laissez-faire*, in the severance of industry from the state, and in the advocacy of natural law in the business world. The line of argument which gives it support also, is as familiar as the philosophy itself. It is assumed that the interests of all are identical and that, on this account, there is no necessity for government to prescribe the conditions of industrial conduct, except so far as they may be prescribed by inference from the established institution of private property. The social interest is either lost to view, or is conceived as nothing more than an aggregate of individual interests.

The modern economist experiences no difficulty in pointing out the error of such reasoning. The individual interest may be, and in some cases is observed to be, at variance with the social interest. Self aggrandizement, a not uncom-

[1][Senior was popularly known as the promulgator of the doctrine that interest was the reward of "abstinence," and as an outstanding opponent of factory legislation. For an able modern reconsideration of Senior, see Marian Bowley, *Nassau Senior and Classical Economics* (London, 1937). This should be supplemented by S. Leon Levy, *Nassau W. Senior* (Boston, 1943). *Editor's note.*]

mon manifestation of self-interest, may, and usually does, set in train forces that are distinctly anti-social. But, fortunately for the world, a negative criticism unaccompanied by constructive suggestions exerts little influence, a truth which applies with especial force to the case in hand. It is not possible for any formal argument to break the influence of that theory of human relations which centers in the needs of the individual man. Individualism is an historic force and not a formal argument. It existed before philosophy undertook its explanation by an appeal to natural law, and it will continue to exist long after the narrow theory of natural law that once gave its support, shall have disappeared. It has been the vital principle of the business code of the English speaking people during the past six centuries. It is bound up in the emancipation of the worker from the restraints of serfdom, in the evolution of property, in the assertion of intellectual liberty, in the development of popular government and in all that goes to make up a society adjusted to the idea of autonomy and spontaneity. It is the essence of that chapter of English jurisprudence which applies liberty to business. It is the sweep of modern history and not the speculations of eighteenth century philosophers, or of nineteenth century economists, which gives sanction to the rule that it is moral for the individual to assert himself. The conditions under which individualism originated, grew, and secured for itself a philosophic expression, must have been such that equity and progress, both social and personal, resulted from its influence, for it could not otherwise have developed. At present, however, the workings of self-interest in the industrial field do not in all respects appear to be in harmony with the ideals of justice, and there are many who profess to see that it places in jeopardy material progress itself. There can be but one explanation of this reversal in the judgment of mankind, and that is, that significant changes have taken place in the industrial conditions to which the theory of individualism is applied. It is, therefore, incumbent upon us to inquire in what particular the industrial present differs from the industrial past, and what modification in the old conception of society is implied in these changed conditions.

The Industrial Revolution, by which tools gave place to machinery and domestic industry was superseded by the factory system, has been so frequently described as to require no further comment. The changes referred to are indeed important, and have set in motion so many and such varied social influences as to justify the name of a Revolution. At the same time it must be admitted that the employment of machinery in the domain of production could not have resulted in the highly differentiated society in which we now live, had it not been for the application of machinery to the service of transportation. We are just beginning, in the closing years of this century, to appreciate the social, industrial and moral significance of railways and steam navigation. It is the modern system of transportation that has revolutionized the world of morals. It is the railway that has destroyed localism in government, in industry, in thought and in interest. It is steam navigation that has created a world's market and removed the chief barrier to the concentration of capital and the growth of great industries. It is the new commercial system that has removed the buyer from the seller, and in so doing, relieved business from the restraining influence of business courtesy. Thus the outlook upon life has been changed. The point of view from which we contemplate human relations has been shifted from the individual to the whole. It is not strange that a revision in the industrial code should have been necessitated by so stupendous a change in the character of industry.

The development of steam transportation also furnishes the stimulus for that movement in morals which characterizes the closing years of the present century. There are those who consider the universal interest in social questions as evidence of a broadening sympathy among men and of an approach toward brotherly kindness. This may be true, but we should be very careful not to plume ourselves upon a righteousness we cannot help. The current interest in social problems results, in large measure, from the fact that we are all sailing in the same boat. The demand for brotherhood is in some degree at least, an expression of the instinct of self-preservation. Were it certain, for example, that a strike or lockout could in no way touch our lives, is it likely we should be so ready to pronounce judgment upon the merits of the controversy? Should we not continue to say, as our forefathers said, that a quarrel to which we are not parties, is of no interest to us? It is because our interests are affected by every industrial quarrel that we are forced to an opinion respecting it. In this fact do we find the characteristic difference between the society of the present and that of an hundred years ago. The rise of socialism and the spread of collectivism are traceable to the increased interdependence among men, and the recognition of society as an organism is traceable to the same fact. All these conceptions of social relations are imposed upon us by external conditions, and it seems clear that a new system of ethics, a new expression of rights and duties, indeed a new definition of liberty and of the individual himself, must be crystallized and incorporated into the established system of jurisprudence, before harmony can be restored between the accepted rule of conduct and these new demands of the moral sense.

There is another event recorded by industrial history which, equally with the substitution of nationalism for localism in industry, shows the necessity of a new interpretation of industrial relations. I refer to the appearance of corporations and to the completeness with which they have transformed the industrial structure. The word corporation opens an almost limitless field of investigation to the student of industrial history, but I shall venture only a few words respecting them, to suggest in what manner the development of this form of association has contributed to the current confusion respecting industrial rights and industrial duties. Corporations originally were regarded as agencies of the state. They were created for the purpose of enabling the public to realize some social or national end without involving the necessity of direct governmental administration. They were in reality arms of the state, and in order to secure efficient management, a local or private interest was created as a privilege or property of the corporation. A corporation, therefore, may be defined in the light of history as a body created by law for the purpose of attaining public ends through an appeal to private interests.

A corporation, as it appears in this latter half of the nineteenth century, differs in every essential particular, from the original conception out of which it grew. Its public purpose and its dependence on government have been lost to view, while its character as a private industrial concern has been especially emphasized. Three points respecting the modern corporation should be noted in order to appreciate the influences which emanate from it.

First. The growth of the corporation and the consequent centralization of industrial power is only limited by the market for the goods which it produces or the services which it renders. This is true because the credit of corporations is practically without limit. The bearing of this fact may easily be perceived. It was assumed by those who formulated the doctrine that the principle of competition was an adequate guarantee of justice and equity in business affairs, that any particular business would be represented by a large number of independent and competing organizations. If, however, what I have said respecting the growth of corporations be true, it is clear that their development tends to destroy the conditions under which competition is alone able to perform its beneficent service.

Second. Corporations are coming to conceive of themselves as business associations of perpetual life. The contracts which they enter into bind not only the present but the future, and, when it is understood that gain in the present is the motive directing these contracts, it is easy to see that the best interests of the future may be jeopardized. I cannot suggest even, at this time, the far reaching consequences of this peculiarity of corporate organization, but must content myself with the remark, that the considerations which led reasonable men of half a century ago to approve the philosophy of industrial individualism, did not include the observation that a body of men organized for the purpose of private gain should ever plead the interests of a perpetual existence. Such a plea, it was assumed, pertained to the state alone.

Third. Corporations do not recognize the principle of

righteousness, candor, courtesy, or indeed, any of the personal virtues, except energy and enterprise, which, according to the old English economists, are assumed to be essential to continued business success. I do not say that the common virtues may not be appreciated by men entrusted with the management of corporate enterprises, or that they do not practice such virtues in their personal affairs; but such is the nature of intercorporate competition, especially for industries in which success is measured by the volume of business transacted, that the managers of corporations are obliged to recognize a dual code of ethics,—one for the business, one for the home. Whether or not a man ought to choose defeat rather than success under such conditions does not concern the present argument. Your attention was called to this peculiarity of corporate organization for the purpose of presenting yet another reason why the old rules of business conduct are not pertinent to the latest phase of industrial development. The old theory of society which assumes identity between personal interests and social morality, may possibly have been true when industries stood forth in the person of those who conducted them; but to claim that this is true as business is at present organized, is to ignore the influence which corporations have exerted upon the character of business. If it be true that the growth of a corporate enterprise is only limited by the world's demands, that its life is only limited by that of the civilization to which it pertains, and that it is deprived of those restraining influences which work so powerfully upon the individual, is it not clear that a new theory of industrial relations becomes a necessity?

For two reasons, then, and they illustrate rather than exhaust the considerations that might be submitted, it seems proper to assert that the theory of social action to which the code of industrial conduct was adjusted by English Economy, no longer describes with accuracy modern industrial society. Localism in industry has disappeared, while simplicity in organization is fast disappearing. The social interest, the social impulse, and the social aim must be more definitely recognized by the formal rules of conduct than was necessary when the locality and the individual were in reality, as well as in theory, the units in the economic order. Under the old individualistic rules of industry, morality centered in the individual life. No opportunity was presented for the evolution of social ethics, no necessity existed for testing motives by their social results. I will not say that the social theory with which this attitude of mind is in harmony was untenable at the time of its development. An opinion upon that point is unnecessary to our purpose. What I do assert is, that the rules of industrial conduct, formulated under such conditions, must fail to take into consideration all the facts of modern industrial life; and one may without serious effort arrive at the conviction that the industrial controversies of our own time are an endeavor to reconstruct the code of ethics that underlies the accepted system of jurisprudence that the social interest and the rights of individuals in associated industry may find a natural and an orderly expression.

II

My second point, designed to show how industrial changes have interfered with the effective working of the accepted system of jurisprudence, pertains to the significance of rights and to the relation between rights and responsibilities. It brings into prominence what is, perhaps, the most fundamental characteristic of social organization, namely: the formula adopted for giving expression to the accepted code of associated action. All peoples who appreciate the stability and protection granted by formal law, express such rules of conduct as they deem wise, either in the language of duty or in the language of right. These concepts, it is true, can not be severed from each other. Every duty implies a right, and every right implies a duty; but this is not equivalent to saying that a society whose laws, judicial procedure, forms of administration, and rules of spontaneous conduct are adjusted to the theory of duty, is the same thing in character, or leads to the same results, as a society which proceeds in its adjustments from the theory of rights. The former, in its fundamental principle is theocratic; the latter is democratic. The conception of law in the former is that of a command imposed; the conception of law in the latter is that of opportunity offered. In a theocracy law finds its sanction in authority and expresses itself as an obligation. Thou shalt not kill; Thou shalt not steal; Thou shalt not bear false witness: such are its legislative expressions. In a democracy, law finds its sanction in the approval of the governed, and expresses itself as a quality inherent in the nature of the case. Man has a right to life, man has a right to property, man has a right to reputation: such is the form of law suitable for a free people.

Nor does the contrast between the two principles of social organization stop here. In a theocracy (and by that I mean any society living under absolute authority—it may be a monarchy) reliance is placed upon the strong arm of the state for the execution of law. The police power comes to be more important as the relations between men become more complex. In a democracy, on the other hand, laws are in a sense self-executory, being expressions of right. Each citizen looks upon government as a protector and appeals to government in case his rights are endangered. Thus law, when approved by the moral sense of the people (and under a mobile democracy nothing else can become law) rests for its execution upon the interested vigilance of all citizens. Each man feels that in the execution of the law his rights are preserved, and that in the development of the law his rights are enlarged.

It is evident that a society organized on the basis of right fits perfectly the requirements of English jurisprudence. It is the design of this system to confine its expression, to general principles fundamental in the code of conduct, and to allow the details of all associated action to be arranged by voluntary association. This is what is meant by the *régime* of contract, and provided the fundamental rights are adequately expressed, and provided also, the conditions are such that the compelling force of responsibility works in the same manner for both parties to the contract, I for one, am willing to trust the safety of the present and the prospects of the future to voluntary association.

It is of the utmost importance, however, that these provisos be met. The rights and liberties expressed must be such as fit into the necessities of the case. The idea of property, for example, cannot be defined with safety by speculation and philosophy, but must adjust itself to the needs of voluntary association, the ultimate aim of association being held in view. The mistake of English political economy, as it seems to me, does not lie in the emphasis it gives to competition as a regulator of commercial conduct, but in its assumption that the *bourgeois* conception of property was ordained by nature and on that account, lay outside the influence of evolutionary forces. But I must set aside for a moment the consideration of this point.

It is also necessary for the satisfactory working of a society whose moral code is expressed in the formula of rights, that responsibility should attach itself to the exercise of liberty. The nature of responsibility must, of course, conform to the nature of the liberty it is designed to control, and dealing as we are with industrial forces, our analysis must content itself, in the application of this principle, with a consideration of industrial responsibility. As already remarked, wherever the system of English jurisprudence holds sway, the details of associated action are the result of voluntary contract, and provided the terms of the contract do not jeopardize any public interest, the state concerns itself only with the task of enforcement.

At this point, however, the analysis must proceed with great care. The word, "enforcement," as employed in English legal procedure, has no thought of arbitrary action. It consists rather in the exacting of the penalty recognized in the contract, (either expressly stated, or implied in the common law under which the contract is drawn) and voluntarily assumed by both parties to the agreement. This exacting of the penalty is the means by which responsibility is brought to the support of voluntary association. Every contract, to be effective, must state or imply not alone the advantages to be secured by the consummation of the agreement, but also the nature and extent, of the loss to be sustained or reparation to be made, in case the agreement is not carried out. The application of this generalization to the industrial controversies of the present time leads to a most important conclusion. It is evident from the nature of the responsibility upon which reliance is placed for the enforcement of contracts, that all parties to an agreement must be commercially responsible; that is to say, they must be in the possession of some property, privilege, or advantage that may be placed in jeopardy as surety for their conduct. The great body of workmen, however, have no property, privilege, or advantage that they can place in jeopardy as a pledge for the fulfillment of a labor contract, from which it follows that labor contracts, on one side at least, are bereft of responsibility, and consequently incapable of enforcement by the orderly procedure of English jurisprudence.

In the situation thus portrayed, do we find the explanation, first, of the reckless manner in which workmen frequently urge their claims; and second, of the tendency on the part of employers to appeal to force. The workmen are reckless because in the evolution of modern industry they have been bereft of all proprietary interest in the plant that gives them employment; the employers appeal to force because there is nothing else to which they can appeal for the restraint of propertyless men. Such is the explanation of the belligerent condition in which the industrial world at present finds itself.

Two or three thoughts are suggested by the above presentation of the situation. In the first place, this turning of the mind toward authority is proof of an incipient infidelity respecting the claims of a free society. It is an admission that the law of property has reached the limit of its evolution, and that it is incapable of giving expression to that refinement of rights which results from differentation in the industrial process. Its logical outcome is the abandonment of the English system of jurisprudence. He who appeals to force turns his back upon a society whose moral code is expressed in the language of rights, and turns his face toward a society whose moral code is expressed in the language of duty.

The second suggestion is, in a sense, the reverse of the one just mentioned. If it be true that the difficulty in the industrial situation arises from the fact that all men come into the industrial order by voluntary agreement, while the majority of men are in no way commercially responsible for the fulfillment of agreement, it is clear that one way of solving the difficulty would be to diffuse commercial responsibility. This, indeed, would be the conservative solution of the problem, for it demands a development within the accepted scheme of jurisprudence rather than a reversal of the established principles of jurisprudence. The truth is, the *régime* of contract cannot work unless all men are in substantially the same condition concerning property; not, I hasten to say, in the amount of property held, but in the relation which proprietorship establishes between the proprietor and industry. To demand, therefore, the diffusion of property, a phrase that I shall explain more fully in a moment, is a conservative demand, for the process it contemplates is essential to the conservation of the *régime* of contract which is the vital principle of liberty in the industrial world.

A third thought is, perhaps, worthy a moment's notice. One who appreciates the above explanation of industrial controversies has little interest in the minor questions that arise respecting the belligerent rights of the contracting parties. How black must be the scowl before it amounts to intimidation? How many men in how many ways may make how many kinds of conspiracy? If a man has a right to be disagreeable to his own employer because of a grievance of his own, has he an equal right to be disagreeable because of the grievance of another worker? Are these not absurd questions? I will not say they are unnecessary, for the rights of belligerents in time of war are of great importance. My point is, that they are uninteresting to the student of economics because they add nothing to the evolution of industrial jurisprudence at the point where evolution is necessary in order to bring industry and law into harmony. The rôle of the economist should be to analyze the situation so as to express these suppressed labor rights, and prepare the way for bringing this period of industrial warfare to a close; and this should be accomplished, not by the enslavement of labor, but by imposing upon labor the responsibility without which liberty is but a name.

III

Let us now turn to a consideration of industrial liberty, which, according to the program laid down, is the third and last point to claim our attention. I shall attempt no definition of liberty, but rest content with the historic prejudice in favor of personal independence and self-realization which is the common possession of all Anglo-Saxon peoples. The liberty of the eighteenth century accepted by the early French and English economists as the background of industrial life, submitted two demands: First, independence in matters of thought; and second, equality of opportunity in matters of action. These demands have in no degree been modified by the subsequent changes in the industrial system; they have rather, been intensified by the growing spirit of democracy. Notwithstanding this, however, a new conception of industrial liberty has been rendered necessary by the needs of a new industrial order. The institution of private property, as defined in the eighteenth century, worked fairly well so long as tools were an appendage to the worker, but it fails to guarantee equality in opportunity now that the worker is an appendage to the machine. The fundamental principle in the theory of Anglo-Saxon liberty is, that the fruits of liberty can be reaped by him alone who has a voice in determining the conditions under which he lives. This is the defense of popular government, and the same argument applies to industrial association. It follows from this line of argument that in the industrial world the possession of property is essential to industrial liberty.

The assertion that property is essential to liberty should be the occasion of no apprehension. It is as old as the conception that the essence of liberty consists in a proper correlation of rights and responsibilties. He who reads with a discerning mind those writers who developed the theory of industrial individualism, will perceive that the ability of a careful and energetic man to acquire property, and through property to control the conditions under which he works, was an assumed, though frequently an unexpressed premise of all their arguments. The same thought underlies the theories of prosperity incorporated into the writings of professed economists. By reference also to the proposals of industrial reformers which have claimed, or are claiming, the attention of our own time, it will be discovered that they all agree in the assertion that it is impossible for a man to become master of himself without acquiring control over the opportunities of labor. What else can the doctrine of the English economists respecting the importance of personal savings imply? What other meaning can be given to the theory of co-operation, the aim of which is to make all laborers capitalists, if it be not that by becoming a proprietor one becomes his own master? How are we to understand the arguments for profit sharing, which urge that one of the perquisites of proprietorship be granted to the worker, except it be assumed that in this manner the worker is made a co-partner with his employer? The same thought lies at the basis of communism, collectivism, and socialism, all of which seek to guarantee men industrial liberty by converting the communal or political organization into an industrial corporation in which all men shall be share holders by virtue of being citizens. We are not concerned with the feasibility of these programmes of reform. They are referred to in this connection because the persistence of an idea is presumptive evidence that it pertains to the conditions out of which it springs; and it is indeed significant that the only ground common to all writers upon social affairs (with the single exception of those who believe in the Tory idea of society) is found in the phrase, that industrial liberty is impossible without industrial property. All recognize, in principle at least, the necessity of a property which shall become an universal possession in order that the character of the worker and the technique of production may conform to the motives of independence and the conditions of self-possession. In no other way can the sense of independence and the sense of responsibility be made universal. In no other way can the fruits of liberty in industry be realized.

But what is this new property, the peculiarity of which is self-diffusion among the workers? This is a question which I admit frankly I cannot answer, but I would not concede it is not worth the asking. It is strictly within the method of scientific investigation to assert the existence of a body or a quality that has not yet been discovered. The astronomer by mathematical reasoning discerns where there must be a planet, and then searches until he discovers it. The chemist arranges compounds in a series, some of which are known, and asserts as a working hypothesis that all exist. In the same manner the economist, after setting in order the mental, the legal, and the psychic forces that make up the industrial life to which history points as the consummation of industrial evolution, is permitted, nay, he is compelled, to assert as a fact which probably exists and which it is reasonable to search for, any element or quality that the furtherance of that evolution demands. The existence of the property right which attaches itself to a citizen of the industrial world in much the same way that political right attaches itself to citizens of a democratic society, is rendered probable by its necessity. Its discovery is essential if liberty and responsibility are to be restored to the industrial order, and on that account its existence may be assumed as a scientific hypothesis for the direction of industrial analysis.

While, however, it is impossible to say that this refinement of property right can at present be defined either in a lawyer's plea, or in the organization of business, three thoughts may be submitted respecting it.

It will, in the first place, rest upon a more perfect analysis of the productive process than the one which leads to the assertion that a man's possessions are the measure of what he or his ancestors added to the world's stock of wealth. It will recognize distinctly and formally the fact of social and associated production. It will rest upon the acknowledgement that one does not fully enumerate the elements of productivity, when to the principle of division of labor described by Adam Smith, and the principle of associated labor groups developed by Mill, he adds the productivity of the entrepreneur function. This function, which is the discovery of modern economic analysis, stands forth in the person of the captain of industry, who, as a business agent, is regarded as a fitful genius of uncertain origin, for whom we should thank God, and to whom we should render payment according to the principle of rent. A new theory always develops slowly, and it is possible that this conception of the captain of industry, projected with such a show of certainty into the discussion of distribution, is a compound of ideas which, when resolved by further analysis into its final elements, will be of assistance in the truthful expression of the respective rights of all parties associated for industrial ends.[2]

Certain it is that association is responsible for an increment of product peculiarly its own. And it is equally certain that no theory of association can satisfy the mind which ignores the slow development of the habit of submission on the part of the great mass of men, without which the captain of industry would be a martinet over a savage hoard; or which ignores the hereditary transmission of aptitudes and skill, which is no unimportant factor in the industrial development of a people; or which ignores the slow accumulation of mechanical knowledge and the crystallization of that knowledge into mechanical inventions; or, indeed, which ignores any of those facts of history or observation that make nationality in industry and prove the race greater

[2][This referred to Francis A. Walker's new theory of interest and profit around which most of the current controversy in economic theory centered. See Adams, "Ten Years of Political Economy in the United States," *Inlander*, 1:23 (March, 1891), and Joseph Dorfman, *The Economic Mind in American Civilization* (New York, 1949), 3:108. *Editor's note.*]

than the man. These suggestions are not new. They are, on the contrary, the common thought of socialist writers, and the fact that they are made the premise of socialist conclusions seems to have led economists who appreciate the grandeur of English jurisprudence to overlook them or to deny them. Such an attitude, however, invites the decay of English jurisprudence. It arrests the development of economic science, and encourages the substitution for it of the science of industrial administration. To deny the fact of social production, and thus preclude the possibility of a development in the idea of property, is not only unfortunate, but there is no justification for it in the nature of the case. Individualism does not consist in living in isolation, but rather in dwelling in a society of recognized interdependencies. Its development is marked by the regress of self-sufficiency and the progress of association. The aggregate of benefits which result from social living is each year traceable in a less degree to what man does, and in a greater degree to what men do. The source of the increment of product is the new relations that men enter into, and not the increase in personal wisdom, skill, or application. The modern productive process is undoubtedly a highly socialized process, but this is no reason why each individual must be swallowed up in society. Provided analysis keeps pace with differentiation so that each specialized social service may be expressed as a social claim, and made the basis of a personal right, the theory of individualism underlying English jurisprudence is as applicable to a complex as to a simple condition of industry. The development of jurisprudence that is needed, therefore, does not pertain to fundamental principles. It must address itself rather to the clarification of those concepts dimly present in all industrial controversies. It is a common law development and not a constitutional change, or a statutory enactment, that is needed. Political economy was brought by John Stuart Mill as far as it was capable of being brought under the eighteenth century conception of property, and the further evolution of industrial theory, as well as the reconstruction of the legal framework of industrial society, must begin with the modification of the concept of property, if any progress is to be made in industrial science or industrial administration.

My second thought respecting that which, by courtesy of your imagination I have termed the workmen's property, is that its clarification will take place through the evolution of collective bargaining and the formal labor contract. Some steps toward collective bargaining have already been taken. Trades-unions are no longer indiscriminately condemned; strikes are no longer considered universally illegal; the law of conspiracy, also, is coming to be confined within its legitimate sphere. At the same time it cannot be said that the situation has been heartily accepted by either party to the controversy. Employers still assert their purpose to bargain with individual employees, and the employees still show a timidity, amounting at times even to cowardice, in the presence of definitely expressed responsibilities. Both appear to think their liberty to consist in being a law unto themselves, rather than in the discovery and measurement of their respective rights in view of the new industrial conditions under which they are obliged to live. Neither appears to recognize that the sociology of the industrial process has rendered collective bargaining imperative, in order that due regard may be paid to the instinct of individualism by which both are impelled. The one thing needed is a true analysis of the situation, and a satisfactory exposition of the advantages that would accrue from the labor contract. This service is the high privilege of economy, but it must be an economy that rests on history, that is motived by a passion for liberty, and that is directed and limited by a knowledge of jurisprudence.

Of the labor contract itself, little can be said with confidence. It is likely that it will provide for determining pay for the work after the work is done; that it will secure to each worker an industrial home; that it will provide for a board of arbitration in each industry. This, indeed, will, in all probability, be its most significant clause, and it is likely that the by-laws of this court of arbitration and the decision which it renders upon such questions as are presented to it, will through a process of natural selection eventually come to be a common law of labor rights. Arbitration thus established would result in a valued possession or privilege of the worker, and on this account he would become a responsible party in the world of industrial association. He would be the proprietor of the rights which the board of arbitration defined.

My third suggestion respecting property rights adjusted to the needs of modern industry is, that the sociology of the industrial process renders it necessary, wherever the interests of society at large are concerned, to lay increased stress upon the theory of industrial agency. This concept is not strange to English jurisprudence, although it has been overgrown, in late years, by the assertions of self-aggrandizement. There is no necessity for the development of a new principle, but rather for the return of an old principle well recognized by common law. The problem to which this thought leads is forced upon our attention by the evolution of corporations, trusts, and great industries; and it is referred to in this connection for the purpose of saying, that the theory of property adjusted to the needs of our time is of a dual character. It must first express the rights of individuals associated together in an industrial unit; it must, next, express the duties of these industrial units to the public at large. The former constitutes the labor problem and the test of its solution should be freedom for the individual to realize himself. The latter constitutes the monopoly problem and the aim of its solution should be the attainment of a just price and the preservation of industrial mobility. Provided these rights can be discovered and expressed in such a manner that they may be incorporated in a contract, on the one hand, and in legislative enactment, on the other, there is no reason in the nature of the case, why harmony cannot be restored to the industrial world, and why the science of Political Economy may not recover that symmetry and form of which it has been deprived by the trenchant criticisms of the last fifty years. As an hypothesis for constructive analysis leading to so desirable a consummation do I offer the suggestions contained in this paper to the members of the American Economic Association.

DISCUSSION OF PRESIDENT ADAMS' ADDRESS[3]

PROFESSOR ARTHUR T. HADLEY, YALE UNIVERSITY:[4] I wish to preface my remarks by expressing my admiration of the way in which President Adams put with so much force many things that we have all been thinking. My suggestion would be that he perhaps put these things with a little too much force, and that there may be a danger in such forcible presentation of thoughts not fully worked out.

My first criticism is historical rather than economic. "It is inseparable," said our President, "from the Anglo-Saxon idea of liberty that the people should have a share in political control." But English constitutional history shows that the idea of liberty was dissociated from the idea of legislative power. The Anglo-Saxon conception of liberty is distinguished by the assurance that precedent will be impartially followed, rather than by the power of those who enjoyed liberty to change such precedents.

Secondly, it is questionable, to my mind, whether the changes in our industrial and economic conditions are as radical as our President holds. There has certainly been some change during the period in question; but the fundamental character of industrial and economic conditions has been the same. President Adams seemed to me to imply that new ideas had recently been introduced into our legal

[3]At the morning session of the Association, December 29, 1896.

[4][Arthur Twining Hadley (1856–1930), Professor of Political Economy (later president) of Yale, had been a fellow member with Adams of Wagner's seminar. He engaged in a methodological controversy with Adams in his "Economic Law and Methods," 1886, reprinted in *Science Economic Discussion* (New York, 1886), pp. 92–97. Hadley was the foremost student of railroads in the United States, but unlike Adams he favored originally advisory rather than "coercive" commissions like the I.C.C. For an excellent biography of Hadley, see Morris Hadley, *Arthur Twining Hadley* (New York, 1948). *Editor's note.*]

system, such, for example, as the perpetual life of corporations. This is open to criticism in that the principle of perpetual succession was well understood and valid in the corporations of the seventeenth century. The East India Company was perpetual, monopolistic, and exclusive to the last degree.

Again, it seemed to me that the evils resulting from the changes in business conditions were too strongly emphasized; and so, also, the suggestion that the separation of buyer and seller in modern corporate enterprise had abolished business courtesy. In practice the old non-competitive or bargaining system is an abominable one. I had much rather deal with the Pennsylvania railroad than a Neapolitan shop-keeper, and should feel much surer of essentially courteous and fair treatment.

What is needed is an accentuation of the principles and tendencies of English jurisprudence: not a new jurisprudence. What the poor man needs is the vigorous and intelligent enforcement of responsibilities, an enforcement which now is often one-sided, partial, and unfair. The President's address seemed to make out a stronger case against the movements of the immediate past than historical tests will warrant. Progress probably will best be made by putting increased emphasis on the side of responsibility. Morals and jurisprudence will best develop by going forward along the old lines; not by going backward to the starting point and then beginning anew in a different direction.

PROFESSOR FRANKLIN H. GIDDINGS, COLUMBIA UNIVERSITY:[5] The President's address seemed to me to be a conservative

[5][Franklin H. Giddings (1855–1931), Professor of Sociology at Columbia University, had been and remained a keen student of economics. See F. H. Giddings and J. B. Clark, *The Modern Distributive Process* (New York, 1888). *Editor's note.*]

view of the policy that industrial communities will have to adopt in order to bring about industrial peace. I understood Professor Adams' chief contention to be that there are easily distinguishable lines of jurisprudence which apply to industrial conditions. One is the absolutist jurisprudence of duties, the other is the democratic jurisprudence of rights. Law as a system of rights is carried out by enforcing contracts, and this is accomplished by putting the property of the contracting parties in jeopardy. Responsibility, in this sense of liability to the loss of property, is the corner-stone of the jurisprudence of rights as distinguished from a jurisprudence of duties. If one of the parties to the contract has no property to be lost when he violates the terms of his contract, his conduct will be rash and contracts will be broken. These conditions often lead to arbitrary conduct by the party who is wronged.

These considerations lead us to seek for that moral or ethical property of the workingman which is not yet recognized in law, but which if recognized could be put in jeopardy by a breach of contract. There is such a property. The law recognizes the right of the worker to demand the payment of a money wage for work done. Does it also recognize the value of a faithful devotion to an employer's interests for a long term of years? As a question of ethics, is not a faithful and self-denying service often an unrequited service? Can it in any way be recognized in law?

If a man has long been a faithful employee, it seems to me that he is entitled to a reasonable notice of impending dismissal, and that the notice should be proportionate to the length of the faithful service. The thing most bitterly complained of by the employees of corporations is the liability to dismissal without notice. Stories of summary dismissals of faithful employees of corporations are common. In lieu of reasonable notification the employee should be entitled to a money damage. Such a right, created by law, would be a form of property. If the employee fails to fulfill his part of the contract, this property right should be forfeited.

PROFESSOR C. S. WALKER, MASSACHUSETTS AGRICULTURAL COLLEGE:[6] I have no criticism to offer on the address of our President, but rise to offer a suggestion in the form of a question. Would it not be possible to have some real tangible property to levy upon in case of breach of contract by the laborer? As it is, in case of such breaking of contract on the part of the corporation, damages can be obtained from the plant and franchise of the corporation. No damages can be collected, however, if the other party, the non-property holding laborer, breaks his contract. But why should not the trades-union to which the laborer belongs have a trust fund, and then as a corporation furnishing labor make a contract with the corporation requiring labor, pledging its fund in case of a breach of contract on its part or on the part of one of its members? Trades-unions are accustomed to keep a large fund on hand from which to pay stipends to men out on a strike and to meet other expenses: why not use a portion for a guarantee?

PROFESSOR L. S. ROWE, UNIVERSITY OF PENNSYLVANIA:[7] The great value of the analysis of economic and legal relations

[6][The Reverend Charles Swan Walker (1846–1933), Professor of Mental and Political Science at the Massachusetts Agricultural College (now the University of Massachusetts), was prominent for his support of agrarian movements. *Editor's note.*]

[7][Professor Leo S. Rowe (1871–1946) held at the time the rank of Assistant Professor of Political Science at the University of Pennsylvania. He was Director General of the Pan-American Union from 1920 to 1946. *Editor's note.*]

contained in the President's address is to be found in the emphasis of certain tendencies which demand recognition in our system of jurisprudence. I shall therefore, confine my remarks to the examination of these tendencies rather than to their practical application.

In the address the contrast between legal principles and industrial relations was approached from the twofold standpoint of the employer and employee. As regards the former the discussion has been confined to the corporate problem. It requires but a cursory glance at the history of corporation law to demonstrate the wide departure from the early idea of the corporation, the idea of an agent of the state endowed with certain of the elements of state prerogative. The logical development of this early idea would have resulted in the enforcement of a strict accountability to the state, which we at present lack. The purely private law concept of limited liability has overshadowed all other considerations. The important point to be noted in this connection is the fact that the consistent application of the "state prerogative" idea would have furnished the legal basis upon which the doctrine of intangible property rights, referred to in the address, and at present represented by the "franchise," might have been further developed.

But how does the question shape itself with reference to the working classes? President Adams dwelt upon the fact that our present system fails to enforce the principle of individual responsibility, as far as the laborer is concerned. This has been due to the fact that up to the present time the basis of enforcement has been the possession of real or personal property of a tangible character. Is it possible to detect any departure from this rule of interpretation in the law of contract? My examination of the subject leads me to believe that such a change is very gradually being effected, at least the way has been prepared. The coercive power of threatened exclusion from certain social opportunities or industrial possibilities; the possibility of exclusion from the benefits of a system of industrial arbitration; from the advantages to be gained through membership in legally recognized labor organizations, may come to form as efficient a means of enforcing individual responsibility against the workingman, as the more tangible property interests of the employer and the intangible "franchises" of the corporation. This development would carry with it the necessity of developing the new class of rights referred to in the address. Viewed in this light—as a question of tendencies rather than a question of practical mechanism—the principles developed in the address must become of great importance in the adjustment of relations in the industrial world.

PROFESSOR HENRY W. FARNAM, YALE UNIVERSITY:[8] The breach of contract most common among wage receivers occurs in the strike, when they deliberately give up their employment. To secure them a new right of employment, and then threaten to withdraw it as a penalty for breach of contract, would be ineffectual, when experience shows that they consider it no serious sacrifice to surrender this very employment in order to carry their point. Such a policy would increase the responsibility not of the wage receiver, but of the employer. Collective bargaining seems to me a more

[8][Henry W. Farnam (1853–1933), Professor of Political Economy at Yale, was a student of Gustav von Schmoller, who was considered the leader of the most extreme wing of the German Historical School. Farnam was especially noted for his generous financial aid for research in American economic history in general and in labor in particular, and for his support of such pioneering organizations in social legislation as the American Association for Labor Legislation. *Editor's note.*]

practical suggestion for preventing breach of contract than the new vague property right suggested.

PROFESSOR GEORGE GUNTON, OF NEW YORK:[9] The idea suggested by Professor Giddings is in operation as a general practice in the factory districts of England. It is a rule throughout Lancashire and Yorkshire, that the laborer cannot be dismissed without notice, except in cases where he spoils his work, or is palpably inefficient. This rule, however, is not regarded with special favor by the laborers; it tends to restrict their freedom of prompt and instantaneous action. The wage classes in general would rather take the risk of summary dismissal than forfeit the right of leaving their employment immediately when dissatisfied. In fact, the introduction of the time notice, and especially of long time notice, has always been regarded as from the employer's side. I remember that in 1875, at the conclusion of the great strike in Fall River, Mass., an iron-clad contract was forced upon the laborers, providing that a notice be required on both sides before the employment could end. If the laborers left without such notice, they were to forfeit the wages due, then in the hands of the corporation, which is a rule that prevails in England. This was regarded by the laborers as a stipulation wholly in favor of the corporation. It would be very difficult to introduce into legislation a rule by which laborers should receive notice before dismissal based upon their fidelity, efficiency and length of service, because no safe rule could be made covering such things. Nor

[9] [George Gunton (1845–1919), who had been a labor leader and active in radical labor movements, was "Professor" in the research organization which he established, The Institute of Social Economics. He became notorious as the leading exponent of the view that uncontrolled "trusts" were a natural outcome of the evolutionary process. *Editor's note.*]

does it seem at all necessary. Such an idea rests on the assumption that in cutting down or otherwise re-arranging the working force, employers select for summary discharge those whose services have been the most efficient and longest. But such is not the case. That would be contrary to the manifest self-interest of employers. Only fools would be guilty of such conduct, and whatever may be said of corporation management in other respects, it cannot be charged that they are economic fools. It is always the inefficient, the irregular, and transient that are to be weeded out, when opportunities arise.

PROFESSOR EDWARD CUMMINGS, HARVARD UNIVERSITY:[10] It may be observed, in passing, that there has been some tendency in this discussion to a mechanical separation and contrast of the economic and the ethical aspects of the question under consideration. It is hardly necessary to insist that such a contrast is superficial; that the conclusions of sound ethics and of sound economics are essentially at one.

On the other hand, the discussion of the mutual responsibility of employer and employees, and of the proposal to remedy the present unsatisfactory conditions by creating for laborers a new kind of property in the right to employment, has presented a very one-sided view of the difficulties of the present situation. While it is proper to emphasize the unquestionable right of trades-unions to exist, and to do business with employers by means of responsible agents, it is equally to be remembered that a great obstacle to improved relations between labor and capital at the present time is the difficulty of finding trade-unions in this country

[10] [Edward Cummings (1861–1926), Assistant Professor of Sociology in the Department of Economics at Harvard, was interested in social ethics. In 1900 he entered the ministry. *Editor's note.*]

which are organized upon business principles, with any such agents ready or able to keep the agreements they claim the right to make. If, therefore, the laborer is to have new rights created for him, he ought also to have new duties: and first of all he ought to assume old duties and responsibilities, inseparably connected with that right to organize upon which he has so strenuously insisted.

Moreover, it is to be borne in mind that there are many reasons why capital has today special claims to protection from the irresponsible organization of labor, as well as labor to protection from irresponsible organization of capital. There are reasons for believing that the heavy burdens of constant industrial reorganization tend to shift more and more upon capital. The rapid march of inventions and improvements in machinery subjects productive investments to greater and greater risk of being superseded and rendered prematurely worthless; while at the same time the loss to superseded skill and labor happily finds at least some compensating tendency in the greater mobility of labor and the shorter apprenticeship which machinery makes possible. Capital, therefore, is deserving of consideration in proportion as its share of necessary waste and cost in industrial progress tends to increase.

It has already been suggested that present conditions would be improved, and responsibility more equally distributed, by some form of contract between the employer and the employees which should provide for adequate deposits of money by both sides, as a pledge of their intention to be bound by the agreement. Such a plan, with the necessary machinery of a joint committee and a standing board of arbitration, has recently been tried in England. It must be confessed, however, that the labor organizations of this country suffer greatly from lack of business-like methods, lack of good leadership, lack of sober intention to undertake the serious business of negotiating with employers for the sale and future delivery of labor. What they need at the present moment is not so much new rights, as a kindly and vigorous insistance upon the assumption of the responsibilities they have already incurred, of duties belonging to the rights they have already secured.

PROFESSOR HENRY CARTER ADAMS: The impression which is left upon my mind by this discussion, and I need not say how deeply interested I am in it, is that there is some danger connected with using old words for new ideas. Professor Commons[11] remarked to me last evening that it seemed to him unfortunate to employ the word "property" in any but the established and accepted meaning. "For," he remarked, "it tends to introduce confusion into a subject that might be presented more clearly by giving specific illustrations of the new rights which laborers are at liberty to urge on account of new industrial conditions." I appreciate very keenly the pertinency of this criticism, and many of the remarks which have been submitted in the course of the discussion this morning emphasize its pertinence. But before consenting that it is unwise to employ the word property in a new sense, it may be well to inquire if the confusion of ideas has been occasioned by my use of this word, or does it exist in the situation itself? As it appears to me, one who analyzes the labor situation at the present time, finds himself groping

[11][John R. Commons (1862–1945) was then Professor of Sociology at Syracuse University. After an interlude of free-lance work, from 1899 to 1904, he resumed an academic post as Professor of Political Economy at the University of Wisconsin, and was the foremost student of American labor. His *Legal Foundations of Capitalism* (1924) is an expansion of Adams's doctrines. *Editor's note.*]

after an idea for which there is no adequate expression. Could it be expressed, however, and become a real thing by being embodied in contracts, it would hold to the laborer the same relation that what we now know as property holds to the proprietor, his employer. If we look at the matter historically, it is clear that the word property has not always meant the same thing. On the contrary, it suggests to the mind a series of rights that have been acquired from time to time; and if the labor problem is in essence what I hold it to be, the social and industrial changes essential for the working out of that problem will add yet another concept to that series of rights and privileges which the past evolution of the English speaking people has crystallized into the word property. At best, one who discusses this problem is reduced to the alternative of using old words with new meanings, or of coining a new word, which could not be understood until explained. For many reasons, I am constrained to believe that, in the long run, greater advantage will accrue from the employment of the word property with a slightly altered meaning than from the coining of any new expression. It is the common method of historic evolution.

It was remarked by one speaker that it seemed to him wiser to follow out in an orderly manner the evolution of society from the point to which it had now come, rather than by retracing our steps to select some other point from which to proceed. The impression seemed to be, though I may have misunderstood the remark, that the address set before itself some mechanical adjustment of labor relations which might be in harmony with a past condition of industry but which found no warrant in the established principles of jurisprudence. If this be the meaning that was intended, I must again plead the apology of a misconception. The only merit possessed by the suggestions contained in the address is found in the fact that they express in language pertinent to the present situation, the principles which have proved themselves adequate in every social crisis sustained by the English speaking people since the thirteenth century.

It is undoubtedly true, as was asserted by yet another speaker, that the burden of modern industry rests upon the shoulders of the employer, while the laborer escapes both the burden and the responsibility. This was fully recognized. It was largely because this is true that the address contended for the creation of a property in the hands of the worker, for in this way only can he become a responsible person in the world of contracts and bear his share of the responsibilities for the orderly administration of industry. Not only is there no liberty for the worker without a property, but there is no stability to industry, unless in some way he is made responsible for the fulfillment of his contracts; and this, as was pointed out, can only result from the possession of some privilege or advantage that he can place in jeopardy.

But I will not continue these remarks. They are but repetitions of what the address has already expressed. I should like to say, however, before taking my seat, that it was not intended to leave the impression that a corporation as an organization was not influenced by the idea of continuity or perpetuity of life previous to the nineteenth century. As a matter of fact the early charters of English corporations were limited to seven years, so that my statement technically was correct. The idea which it was intended to convey, however, was that in the nineteenth century for the first time have men, associated together for private business ends, accustomed themselves to regard their association as a body of continuous life. This fact of continuity is doubtless inseparable from a corporation, and it is largely because this is true that we cannot consent to the opinion that a corporation can be a purely private affair.

Permit me to thank the members of the Association for the interest which they have shown in this paper and for the courtesy with which they have discussed it.

Acknowledgments

THE EDITOR acknowledges with gratitude the generosity shown by the following in making the publication of the Bicentennial Editions and Studies possible: the Trustees of Columbia University, the Trustees of the Columbia University Press, Mrs. W. Murray Crane, Mr. James Grossman, Mr. Herman Wouk, and friends of the late Robert Pitney who wish to remain anonymous.

In obtaining materials the following organizations have been especially helpful: the Columbia University Libraries, the Cornell University Library, the Alumni Office and the Library of Johns Hopkins University, the Michigan Historical Collections of the University of Michigan, the New York Public Library, the Rochester Public Library, and the State Historical Society of Wisconsin. Professors Solomon F. Bloom, of Brooklyn College, and Z. Clark Dickinson, of the University of Michigan, have been of considerable aid in various ways. I wish also to thank Miss Irene M. Davis, Registrar of Johns Hopkins University, who gave me the lead to the valuable material in the University Alumni Office.

Index

APPENDICES

APPENDIX 1

AN INTERPRETATION OF THE SOCIAL MOVEMENTS OF OUR TIME.

It is my purpose to interpret in this lecture,[1] so far as it lies in my power, the social movements of our own times. In undertaking such a task, it is necessary at the outset to choose between two ways of thinking on what is happening about us, or, stated in a personal manner, between two classes of thinkers.

On the one hand, there are those who profess to explain the unrest in modern society by referring it to the spirit of jealousy on the part of those whose possessions are small, and to the love of power and aggrandizement on the part of those who force their way into leadership. "There is no just ground for complaint," exclaim these self-appointed representatives of the great middle class. "Are not workmen, as a whole, better off than they once were,—do they not have more to eat and more to wear,—are not prices cheaper and wages higher? Why, then, should they complain? It is envy which leads them to complain, —it is ambition that voices their complaint. What they need is a parson or a prison, and it makes little difference which."

I do not care to say a word respecting this interpretation of social unrest. My opinion is that the increase of material comforts for the great mass of men is less than many seem to think; but for this morning I purpose bringing the discussion upon a higher plane. The life is more than meat. The benefits of a civilization are not synonymous with an appeased appetite. The cause of discontent lies in the minds of men, and the source of unrest

[1]This paper was given before the School of Applied Ethics, at Plymouth, Mass., August 12 [1891] being the closing lecture of a six weeks' course on the History of Industrial Society and Economic Doctrine in England and America.

is found in the aspirations of men. A social movement is not explained by saying that agitators take advantage of the spirit of envy to stir up strife. A great man is he who voices the will of the people; he cannot construe that will. A successful leader is one who points the way by which a popular ideal may be realized; he cannot create the ideal. "No man can make a revolution," exclaimed Lasalle, that prince of revolutionists, and he was right; a social movement must spring from the conditions in which men live.

From such assertions you may readily appreciate that I ally myself with those who hold that a social movement is sure to arise whenever there is a lack of harmony between the realities of life and the ideals of living. It becomes my duty, therefore, in undertaking to interpret the social movement of our own times, to disclose, first, those changes in industrial methods by which harmony in industries has been disturbed, and then to trace the influence of such changes into the structure of society. In this manner we shall discover, I think, that we are dealing with a permanent historical force, and not with a passing whim.

In seeking to understand modern industrial society, it is necessary to go back to the last quarter of the last century, and inquire respecting the changes that have taken place in the processes of industry. We are in these days so accustomed to the use of machinery, and so familiar with great industries, that it is difficult to picture a society in which tools were used and in which industries were small. Yet it is scarcely a hundred years since the era of inventions began. In the textile industry, for example, at the time when Adam Smith wrote his great work, *The Wealth of Nations*, the manufacture of cloth was but four steps removed from most primitive methods. Thus, the distaff had given way to the spinning-wheel; a fulling machine had come into use, by which the boys and girls were relieved from tramping about with bare feet on the cloths thrown into a running stream; a frame for holding warp had been contrived, and the flying shuttle invented. This short list completed the list of inventions which the history of the textile industry records from the Trojan war to the vandalism of Napoleon. Penelope would have been qute at home among the textile workers of the last century in England.

The flying shuttle, invented in 1738, was a contrivance as important as it was simple. It consisted of two springs fastened to the loom in such a manner that the weaver could easily snap the shuttle from side to side. Not only did this increase the efficiency of his work, but it relieved him from the most tedious part of his labor. Before this he had been obliged to bend first to the right, and throw the shuttle through, and then to the left, and throw it back again. Is it not remarkable that for centuries men should have endured the fatigue of such unnatural labor, when, by means of a hickory stick and a hempen string, and so much of ingenuity as a Yankee calls into play every day of his life, the difficulty could have been easily overcome. I bring this to your notice for the purpose of illustrating the fixedness in industrial habits.

But with the year 1760 all this was changed. It happened that a weaver by the name of Hargreaves, coming home late one night, pushed the door of his cabin suddenly open, and toppled over the spinning-wheen at which his wife sat at work. She, doubtless accustomed to such sudden entrances, did not scream or drop the yarn, and the spindle, although thrown into a perpendicular position, continued its merry hum. A bright idea flashed into the mind of the weaver: if the good wife had a dozen hands she could spin a dozen yarns at once; and upon this idea it is that England has since built her commercial and manufacturing greatness. The machine which Hargreaves invented was called the Spinning-Jenny; some say because his daughter's name was Jenny, some say because his wife's name was Jenny, while others declare it was in honor of a neighbor's wife. The exact truth regarding the domestic relations of Jenny we do not know, but of one thing we are certain, the name of this female will not be forgotten as long as people wear cottons and woollens.

This invention was the first of a long series of inventions which resulted in an industrial revolution, and the difficulty is for us to appreciate that so small a thing could bring about a revolution. You have doubtless seen a child playing with his blocks upon the floor, setting up one after another in a row. So long as no accident occurs they all stand, but should the skirt of the child or a breeze from the door topple one of them over, they all fall. So it is with industries before disturbed by the restless genius of the nineteenth century. Somehow, trades had been established,—the spinner, the weaver, the fuller, and the dyer. Somehow, accustomed methods of work had been set up. Somehow, men had adjusted themselves to certain ways of doing business. The son entered the trade of his father, and the father taught the son rules of trade that had been followed for generations. Precedent was thus crystallized into habit, and the thought of change in the methods of work did not enter the minds of men. Thus for centuries, if we except agriculture, the habits of workmen remained unchanged.

It was into such a society as this that the accident of Hargreaves's invention was thrown. The spinning-jenny increased the efficiency of the spinners a hundred-fold, and thus gave the weavers more yarn than they could weave. The adjustments that had grown up with centuries were destroyed in a moment. It was essential that yarn spun by machinery should be woven by machinery and the power-loom, thus becoming a necessity for society, was quickly invented. But economy in the use of machinery demands the best power for driving machinery,—a demand which was met by what is commonly known as the invention of the steam-engine, but which was merely the refitting of an old model that up to this time could have had no profitable commercial use had it been perfected. These are but illustrations of how one process of work depends upon another, and how a change in one part of industry demands a change throughout. It would be futile for me to mention even all the inventions of this era of invention. The spinning-jenny was followed by the water-frame, by roller-spinning, the power-loom, the engine, the safety-lamp (without which the engine could not have been supplied with coal), chemical bleaching, printing in colors from rollers, and I know not what else besides; but this genius for invention did not cease until, upon the ruins of the old domestic system of industry, there had been established what we now know as the factory system.

The most apparent of the results following upon the changes referred to is the marked increase in the efficiency of labor; but to measure that increase is by no means a simple task. It is reflected in the rapid expansion of population which began with 1790. But figures are dry and uninteresting. It is observable also in the increased exports and imports, in the growth of property values, in the number of factories built, in the number of miles of railway opened. But again we say that figures are dry, and, more than that, they are an unknown language to those not familiar with them.

Fortunately, there is another method more interesting in itself by which the increased efficiency in labor may be clearly expressed. The secret of the productiveness of modern methods of industry is that the forces of nature have been brought under the control of man. Thus it may be said that our industrial system is founded on coal, for it is this which permits man to bring such tremendous forces to his assistance. There is in a ton of coal latent energy equal to eleven million times its own weight, one-eleventh of which is rendered available by means of the ordinary steam-engine. This means that a miner in Pennsylvania who digs five tons of coal a day gains for society what is equivalent to five million tons of energy, and this he does for one dollar and fifty cents.

The most surprising results are observed when we trace the use of coal in the transportation of goods. A cube of coal which will pass through a ring the size of a twenty-five-cent piece will carry a ton of cargo two miles on its ocean voyage. A ton of freight may be drawn a mile on a railway by the burning of two ounces of coal. It is said there is carbon enough in a postage-stamp to carry a letter on its average journey. Is it, then, any occasion for surprise that the world is growing rich when nature's forces thus serve the industrial purposes of men?

We might also measure the effect of new methods of work by estimating the increased efficiency of labor in the textile industry. For example, it was possible for a man to weave by hand from forty-two to forty-eight yards of cloth in a day. Now, one man can tend power-looms and weave fifteen hundred yards of cloth in a day. The effect of machinery in agriculture is no less surprising. In our own country, seven men can grow, mill, bake, and distribute bread enough to feed a thousand. The last estimate on this point, however, is that of Carroll D. Wright. In 1880 there were in the United States fifty millions of people, but they produced an amount of value which would have required the labor of two hundred and twenty-seven millions of people working under the old methods, and this estimate does not take into account the increased population to supply the demand for increased food.

My only purpose in presenting such facts as the above is to leave upon your minds the impression that important changes have taken place in business methods and in mechanical appliances. There is greater difference between 1790 and 1890, in all matters of business procedure, than between the twelfth century and 1790. Arnold Toynbee is right in calling this stupendous change an industrial revolution.

But if a revolution, what has been its effect on society? Upon the difficult task of answering this question, I scarce know how to enter. We are dealing with the forces which give character to the nineteenth century. In a sense, indeed, we are bringing the nineteenth century to trial. The stern, unyielding spirit of commerce has gained for men the possibility of a higher and a fuller life. Do we realize the possibilities of that life, or are we like a man who, having built a fine house, is content to live in the kitchen?

Although the interpretation of this revolution in methods of industry is a difficult task, we may at least approach it in a simple manner. Resisting the invitation to indulge in grand generalization, I ask your attention to three questions. First, what does the industrial revolution mean for the workingman? Second, what does it mean for the statesman? Third, what interpretation may be placed upon it by the scholar? By this manner of approach we may gain a complete statement of the case. For, from the laborer we may learn what class interests are involved; from the statesman we may discover what public interests are placed in jeopardy; while the scholar, standing apart from any special interest, will be able to tell us whither the struggling forces of the nineteenth century are urging our civilization.

The appropriate answer to the first of these questions is suggested by the fact that a laboring class was born out of the changes which made modern society what it is. This appears to be paradoxical. Why should the invention of machinery, the object of which is to save labor, have resulted in the creation of a laboring class? The meaning of my statement, however, becomes clear when it is learned that by the phrase "laboring class" is not meant a class of men who labor, but a class of men who, having no property in anything but themselves, are obliged to seek an opportunity for working from those who are the proprietors of the agencies of production. It is true that in agriculture there had come to be the germ of a laboring class, but in the textile industries, in the hardware industries,—indeed, in all the trades,—there was no decided separation between employers and employés. The master and wage-earner worked side by side; both had served the same apprenticeship; and most frequently the workman was a member of the family of his master. And since no great amount of capital was required to set up a competing business, the earnings of the master could be at no time much higher than the wages of his journeyman. The point to be held in mind is that all who had to do with industries were workers, and the workers, therefore, were able to control the conditions under which they worked.

But when machinery came to be used, all this was changed, and there sprang into existence a class of proprietors over the mechanism of production, and all others engaged in manufacturing pursuits were forced to come to these proprietors for employment. Many years did not pass before a complete separation took place between these two classes. The factory system gradually arose, and by its growth independent workers were forced to the wall. There was thus created a great class of non-possessors who depended upon daily wages for the means of livelihood. Under the old system, these men were proprietors of the material on which they worked, of the tools with which they worked, and of the houses in which their work was carried on. But under the factory system, they are proprietors of nothing. They work in a building owned by their employers, upon material owned by their employers, with machines owned by their employers. This, then, was what was meant in saying that the development of machinery had given rise to a distinct laboring class. It is the reverse of the statement that the industrial revolution has given rise to a distinct capitalist class. It means that the industrial community of this century for the first time is divided into possessors and non-possessors, whose interests seem to be identical so far as production is concerned, but whose interests are opposed to each other when questions of distribution come up for settlement.

This same fact may be presented more vividly in another manner. Did you ever think of the difference between a tool and a machine, and endeavor to understand why a society based on tools must be unlike a society based on machinery? A tool is an implement which enables a man to use to better advantage the strength that lies within him. It may be regarded as a newly-added organ by means of which his physical powers are more efficiently expended. A machine, on the other hand, is an implement or a mechanism which enables a man to bring under his control those forces external to himself. When working with machinery, or, as it is sometimes called, with capital, a man no longer relies on the force within him,—he reduces to servitude the forces without him. Now it is plain that in a society based on tools the element of labor is relatively of more importance in production than the element of capital, from which it follows that the workmen are in a position to control the conditions under which they work. But in a society based on machinery, human power is not the most important factor. It is control over the forces of nature that now measures the degree of industrial efficiency, and it follows that they who own the machinery through which natural forces work are able to determine the conditions of industry. This, then, is the significance of the change from tools to machinery. In a society adjusted to manual labor, it is absolutely impossible that a labor problem, as a class problem, should take its origin; but in a society adjusted to machinery, provided the English law of property be maintained, the development of class lines will surely make its appearance in industries.

Holding in mind the comparison thus brought to our notice, we are in a position to state in a sentence what the industrial revolution means for the laboring class. It means that the worker has lost control over the conditions of labor, and the labor agitation of our own times, so fearful in its tendencies, so demoralizing in the bitterness of hatred engendered, is but the effort of workingmen to gain again control over the conditions in which work shall be done.

We now come to consider the meaning of the industrial revolution for the statesman, or, to present the question as stated above, to ask what new duties are imposed upon government by the industrial changes which have taken place. The appropriate answer to this question is suggested by recurring to a well-known historical fact. The characteristic difference between industrial life in the Middle Ages and in the nineteenth century is that in the former period competition did not exist,—

it was not allowed to exist, for law, or custom having the force of law, impeded its workings at every step. But by the last half of the eighteenth century most of the laws regulating business had become inoperative. Indeed, more than this is true. Not only had men freed themselves from the old restraints, but they had come to believe that in competition society had discovered a principle of control which, while inviting progress, secured justice. Thus, the practice of individualism was converted into the philosophy of individualism; a new social principle was accepted in place of the old.

All this is familiar to every student of history, but there is one fact which seems to have been overlooked. At the time when individualism in industry was promulgated by Adam Smith, industries were small and widely diffused. Men were using tools, and the business relations were personal and direct. Under such conditions there is greater likelihood that competition would work with equity than at the present. But without attempting to develop this thought, let me call your attention to the significant fact. The truth is, the theory of industrial liberty, framed to meet a *régime* of hand-work, has been accepted and developed by a society which knows only machine labor. A social philosophy adjusted to a scheme of domestic industry has been maintained, notwithstanding the fact that domestic industry has given way to the factory system. There is no better illustration in the whole range of history of the illogical application of a social principle. The privileged classes in the nineteenth century have no right in reason, or in honesty, to urge in defence of their privileges a principle that took its origin in a society whose destruction was the occasion of their birth.

We are not, however, concerned with the ethics of history, nor have we time to follow out the abuses arising from this mal-adjustment of a social principle to social conditions. The question in hand pertains to the meaning of the industrial revolution for a statesman, and this is surely indicated by what has been said. A statesman knows, or should know, that a nation cannot expect a healthful growth when the philosophy of rights and duties on which its laws are based is out of harmony with the every-day life of men; and it becomes his duty, as the guardian of rights and the formulator of law, to work to restore harmony in the social organism. When, shortly after the independence of the colonies, Thomas Jefferson became Governor of Virginia, he set before himself the task of reorganizing the colonial government to meet the necessities of a free commonwealth. So, the statesman of to-day, recognizing the industrial revolution to be an accomplished fact, should set before himself the task of so adjusting the structure of government, and of so modifying the law of industrial rights and duties, that symmetry in structure and harmony in rights may be realized for modern society.

It is possible to present this thought a little more definitely. The period intervening between 1790 and 1830 in England, was a period of social disintegration, and the suffering of the dependent classes, on whose shoulders the burdens of change rested most heavily, was so great as at last to arouse the ethical sense of society. Many who themselves did not feel the burdens of change, but awakened by sympathy for the degraded condition into which English workingmen had fallen, exerted all their energies to alleviate the suffering about them. It was the degradation of the English laborer that gave rise to a school of workers and writers known as Christian socialists. The names of Frederick Maurice and of Charles Kingsley are sufficient to suggest the sweetness and light which permeated its teachings. The attention of English philanthropists was first drawn to the condition of children in factories. If you would know the horrors to which children were subjected by unregulated competition in the production of cottons, read the description which Harriet Martineau has left in her "History of England." It was for factory children that Elizabeth Barrett Browning wrote that stanza so often quoted, a stanza full of impassioned pathos to one who knows the state of affairs which brought it forth.

> "Do ye hear the children weeping, O my brothers,
> Ere the sorrow comes with years?
> They are leaning their young heads against their mothers,
> And that cannot stop their tears.
> The young lambs are bleating in the meadows;
> The young birds are chirping in the nest;
> The young fawns are playing with the shadows;
> The young flowers are blowing towards the west,—
> But the young, young children, O, my brothers,
> They are weeping bitterly.
> They are weeping in the playtime of the others,
> In the country of the free."

I should not have drawn your attention to the philanthropists were it not that the legislation to which their efforts gave rise is typical of what government can do. The truth is, competition has not worked in the nineteenth century as Adam Smith, writing for the eighteenth century, said it would work. Shall we on that account abandon it and return to those minute regulations of early England? This is the alternative which presents itself to many, but I imagine the question is not one of unbridled industrial license or of complete governmental control, for either of these methods leads to tyranny. There must be a middle course which leads to industrial liberty. Much that has been said in favor of competition is beyond controversy. Mobility of movement is essential to a highly-developed society. Without personal liberty there can be no hope, and hope is the only abiding motive to action. But we make a sad mistake if, from such a premise, we exclude the sovereign power of the state from the industrial field. That is not the best government which governs least, but which governs the most wisely.

Consider now in what a position the changes of the last one hundred years have left the statesman. Forced to admit the benefits of competition, and at the same time to admit that competition fosters evils, he is obliged to trace with faltering step a path lying midway between the policy of action and the policy of inaction. He must decide under what conditions competition works well and see that for those conditions its actions are unimpeded; he must, on the other hand, determine under what conditions competition works badly, and either regulate its actions by law or exclude it altogether.

From this it appears that there are at least two lines of policy upon which government may enter:

First, government must regulate the plane of competition, for without legal regulation the struggle between men for commercial supremacy will surely force society to the level of the most immoral man who can sustain himself. The fittest to survive unregulated competition will be he who is morally the least fit to live. For purpose of illustration,[2] suppose ten manufacturers competing with each other to supply the market with cottons. Assume that nine of them, recognizing the rights of childhood, would gladly exclude from their employ all but adult labor. But the tenth man has no moral sense. His business is conducted solely with a view to large sales and a broad market. As child labor is actually cheaper than adult labor, he gives it a decided preference. What is the result? Since his goods come into competition with the goods of the other manufacturers, and since we who buy goods only ask respecting quality and price, the nine men whose moral instincts we commend, will be obliged, if they would maintain themselves in business, to adopt the methods of the tenth man, whose immoral character we condemn. Thus the moral tone of business is brought down to the level of the worst man who can sustain himself in it.

What, now, can government do in such a case? One of the duties of government is to express and enforce the ethical sense of society, and in this case government may, acceding to the wishes of the nine manufacturers, pass a law saying that

---

[2]This illustration is taken from my pamphlet entitled *The State in Relation to Industrial Action.* [This is the first essay printed above.]

children shall not be employed in factories. By such interference, society is not deprived of the advantages of competition, but the plane of competition is adjusted to the moral sense of the community. Such, at least, is the dfence of factory legislation, and such interference on the part of government is typical of a new line of duties which the development of great industries has imposed upon the statesman of the nineteenth century.

The second class of duties imposed on government by the changes which have come over modern business life are of a wholly different character. There are some industries which from their very nature are superior to competition, and for such the public has no guarantee of fair treatment. It is absurd to argue that commercial laws will insure equity in the dealings of railway companies, telegraph companies, electric-lighting companies, street-railway companies, and the like. It lies in the structure of such businesses to be conducted as monopolies and in disregard to the comparative rights of men. The important point for us to hold in mind, however, is this: The existence of monopolies proves the existence of an anti-social interest. It shows that the interest of individuals is not always identical with that of the public. Now government stands for public interest, and, among the new duties imposed on government by the industrial revolution which we have described, is the duty of protecting citizens against the encroachments of such monopolies as are the fruit of that revolution.

We have thus answered directly the question, what new duties the changes in modern life have imposed on government. These duties are two. First, the government must determine the plane on which competition may take place in those businesses in which it is potent. Second, it must by all possible means protect the community from those evils that arise from the uncontrolled management of a business, which from the nature of the case is superior to competition.

We come, then, in the third place, to inquire what meaning this wonderful social and industrial change has for the scholar.

As already remarked, the scholar differs from either the laborer or the statesman when contemplating modern society, in that he is not retained to represent any particular interest. He views the movements of society as it were from a height, and, though his mastery of detail may not be as complete as that of the laborer or the statesman, he will be more apt than they to discover the general trend of events. History to him is like a river lying at the base of a mountain on which he stands. He can see whence it comes from among the upland hills, he can see whither it is flowing on towards the sea. It is, then, a wholeness of view that we have a right to expect from the student. And on this account, what he says, if he be a truthful watchman on the mountain, must be of use to those whose closer connection with the affairs of life does not permit so broad an outlook.

When considering the social movement from the stand-point of the laborer, it might have been stated that trade organizations appeared to him necessary for protection. He felt rather than understood the evils which machinery brought, and joined hands with fellow-workmen for resistance. This suggests a very interesting question, and one that will serve as a key to the scholars' view of social movements. Does the rise of trades-unions bear any peculiar significance, or is it to be regarded merely as an outcry from those upon whose shoulders the burden of industrial development rested most heavily? To this question I will give a direct answer. In my opinion, combination among workingmen is a necessary step in the re-crystallization of industrial rights and duties. From the sixteenth century to the beginning of the nineteenth century, the tendency has been towards disintegration in all matters of property and industries. In early society, when men worked wholly for local markets, when the relation between employer and employé was a personal relation, competition was kept in restraint by custom and by law. But with the downfall of feudalism, with the discovery of the new world, with the new spirit of personal independence infused into life by the great religious reformation and by the political struggles, all this was changed. Localism gave way to nationality, competition took the place of custom, and wealth came to be used as capital. It was at this point in the development of English society that the era of inventions made its appearance, and the result was what might easily have been expected. The power and the energy previously shown in religious and political controversies now made itself manifest in trade. Great industries sprang into existence, and under the theory of property then prevalent it naturally followed that the new social power generated by the use of machinery fell into the hands of those who were so fortunate as to become proprietors of the mechanism of production.

This is a most important fact if we would understand the industrial armament in which the world stands to-day, for it shows that the concentration of industrial power did not begin with the workmen when they organized themselves into unions, but was an inevitable result of the use of machinery in a society whose legal structure was shaped to meet the conditions of personal competition. It began when employers came to be exclusive proprietors of machinery, of material, and of factory. My point is this. The birth of a capitalist class, freed from the restraints formerly imposed by custom and law, was the first step in industrial armament, while the organization of labor into unions of trades is to be regarded as a second step, a counter-movement on the part of those whose interests were endangered by the rise of great industries. This is the historical explanation of trades-unions.

Did you ever ask under what conditions it is possible for competition to work justly? "A fair bargain," says Professor Clark, "demands either a desire for justice on the part of the participants, or strategic equality between them."[3] Now, for

[3][This was Professor John Bates Clark and the quotation is from his *The Philosophy of Wealth* (Boston: Ginn, 1886, 2nd ed., 1887, p. 132.]

fifty years after the introduction of machinery there was no approach to the realization of either of these conditions. Wherever the doctrine of *laissez-faire* holds sway (and it held sway during the fifty years we are considering) an effective desire for justice is impossible. Indeed, according to the doctrine, it is absurd to strive for justice in business affairs, for, according to the doctrine, justice must result from the interplay of self-centred motives. Nor was there strategic equality between the sellers and the buyers of labor. The ability to control the conditions of work lay wholly with the employers. An individual workman was swallowed up and overwhelmed in the vortex of competitive forces. Laborers found that they had lost the importance which they formerly enjoyed, and it was to recover their lost ground that they organized themselves into unions. It was to obtain strategic equality with their masters that they entered into combinations. It was to mass their brute force against the brute force of machinery that they submitted to the military discipline of trade organizations. Thus the growth of trades-unions is to be regarded as a counter-movement, not an aggressive movement. It marks the second step in the crystallization of industrial power, not the first step.

Of course you will ask what will be the outcome of this industrial armament in which the Christian world now lives. That question cannot be answered. What the future has in store is known only to Him who holds the destiny of nations in his hands. But of one thing we may be sure. Unless some way be discovered by which the deep ethical purpose of society can be brought to bear upon industrial questions, our magnificent material civilization will crumble to ashes in our hands. Some advocate the destruction of trades-unions. Stop organization among workmen, they cry, and all will go on in harmony and quiet. I will not stop to show that this would bring back the state of affairs existing in the first quarter of the century, which resulted in forcing the workman to the bottom of the abyss. Such a proposal is childish, for the thing proposed is impossible.

As well might we call on the waters of the Niagara to roll back. Organization is the most potent fact in the industrial history of the nineteenth century, and it must either be used for the good of society or society must bear the ills which it brings.

The only practical question, then, asks how to use organization. One hears a great deal these days about the relation of ethics to economics. Certainly many foolish things have been said on this point, but at bottom the talk rests on the eternal truth that a peace born of justice can never be realized by balancing brute force against brute force. And yet this is what the men who control the business affairs of to-day are endeavoring to do. To my mind, the ethical sense of society must be brought to bear in settling business affairs. Indeed, I am willing to go further. In many cases the ethical principle must supplant the competitive principle, and it is an encouraging thought, to say the least, that possibly the growth of organized labor has provided the machinery by which this may be done. Above the interest of the contending parties stands the interest of the public, of which the state is the natural guardian, and one way to realize the ethical purpose of society in business affairs is by means of legislation to bring the ethical sense of society to bear on business affairs. Such a statement, of course, opens up a wide field of discussion. I will only say, in illustration of my meaning, that the long list of statutes known as factory acts, by which the plane of competition is legally determined, or the establishment of commissions whose duty it is to guard the interests of the public when endangered by the growth of monopolies, are to be regarded as the legal expression of the ethical sense of society.

Laws of this sort, however, do not touch the labor problem. That problem has to do with the rights and duties under which work shall be done. Its solution, then, is beyond the law. The object held in view by the workmen, when they organized themselves into unions, was to gain again that control over the conditions of labor which they lost when machinery took the place of tools. How such an end will be attained we cannot say. Some advocate co-operation, others urge the extension of the principle of profit-sharing, while still others seem to think all difficulties would disappear should wages fluctuate with the price of goods. We must pass these proposals without discussion. A thought of more promise, as it appears to me, but by no means as familiar, is that the prevalent tendency towards crystallization of industrial power should be carried one step further, until employers and employés are all to be found in the same organization. This is a simple idea, but it is far-reaching in its tendencies. Its realization would require that employers should recognize unions and deal with the men in a body; that they should be willing to submit all matters of internal organization to arbitration; that men already employed in industry should have preference over men outside; and, what is perhaps of most importance, all these should come to the workingmen as their right, and not by the grace of employers. This seems like giving up everything to the workmen, and it would indeed result in a new form of industrial organization in which the wage-earner would receive greater consideration. But it would, I am sure, increase rather than decrease the efficiency of industry and be of mutual advantage to all concerned.

Without attempting to develop the idea thus suggested, let me, in closing, bring the social movement of our time into harmony with the observed tendencies of modern industry.

In matters of religion and government the characteristic tendency of modern history has been towards the development of personal liberty. The power of organized dogma has given way before the assertion of the individual to think for himself, and the doctrine of the divine right of kings has been supplanted by the theory of representative government. Now it requires no very profound study to see that the theory on which industries are organized is not in harmony with the theory realized in the other departments of our democratic society. The actual control over industries lies with those who possess property.

There is no industrial liberty for those who possess no property, except the liberty to seek employment. The idea which now maintains with regard to industrial rights is analogous to the idea entertained by Charles I. with regard to political rights. The question at issue between this king and our Puritan ancestors was: Is control over political power a right or a grant? It is a right, said the English ruler, and I will exercise it as I please. It is a grant, said the Puritan, and you will please to exercise it as we will. You are familiar with the result, and how out of the controversy responsible government was established.

Now it seems to me that the social movement of our own times is a movement of the same sort. The power which men of property now claim they have the right to use in an irresponsible manner is the power generated by the development of machinery. But this claim is denied by the great class of non-possessors. The power of capital, it is asserted, is a social power, and the laws of property which grant irresponsible control over it to individuals are unjust laws. Thus, the question which now confronts the industrial world is this: Is control over industrial power a right or a grant; are capitalists proprietors or are they agents? No one can say how these questions will be answered; but if the future may be read from the past, and if the spirit of history regards either logic or equity, it requires no great intellectual courage to assert that the social movement of our own times will not rest until there has been established in supreme authority that triumvirate of ideas, Religious Liberty, Political Liberty, and Industrial Liberty.

APPENDIX II

CORRESPONDENCE

Ithaca, N.Y., March 25, 1886

Dr. James B. Angell,
University of Michigan, Ann Arbor, Mich.

My dear Sir:-

I will undertake a reply to the questions contained in your favor of the 19th, though of necessity my statements must be very short.

1. You ask to what extent I question the right of private property. My theory of property rests upon the thought that the only tenable defense of property is its necessity. The final right of control over all productive agencies lies with society, and a proprietor should always be regarded as an agent who manages for a principal. The question, therefore, as to how far men should be permitted to control productive agents as though they had a final right in them, is wholly a question of expediency, that can be answered only by experiment and the common sense of men.

To answer the question more specifically with regard to land, it seems to me best to permit agricultural lands to remain as at present the private property of individuals; but at the same time I would limit its possible accumulation in the hands of single individuals. The extent of that limit is a technical question of agriculture. But on the other hand, city real estate used for rentals, (that is ground rents, not capital invested in buildings) does not appear to me a just object for private ownership. The same is true of those funds of gratuitous wealth stored up from the past, unless they be so widely diffused that the public has a guarantee in competition that they will be furnished at the necessary cost of appropriation. Pine lands and copper mines are examples of this sort of wealth. I of course will not burden my statement with questions of method.

Capital differs from land in that it is produced and not a gratuitous gift of nature. The question of importance, so far as the expediency of granting individuals complete control over it is concerned, is,—Whether capital is an individual or a social product. Or perhaps the better way to put the question would be,—Upon which hypothesis may we hope to realize the greater degree of justice to all men engaged in industry? I am aware that the distinction here suggested is not a familiar one, but at the risk of being misunderstood, I will say, that my own reasoning rests upon the assumption that capital is a social product. How then may it be managed so that society shall realize most perfectly its highest purposes? In answer to this query, two proposals present themselves. The one holds that since capital is a social product, the state should own and control it. That is state socialism and from this I dissent. The other proposal is, that since capital is a social product, control over it (that is, property in it) should be so widely diffused that all members of society may enjoy the benefits that flow from it. This is the view I accept, but at the same time I hold that as industries are at present organized, and as law and custom now interpret the rights that come with proprietorship over capital, it is impossible to realize this purpose. The solution of the social problem lies in the discovery of some way by means of which this end may be attained, and I am convinced that no solution is possible that will not disappoint the selfish expectations of many who now look upon their property in capital as a thing of personal right. When your letter came, there was lying on my table an article that I had just written touching this point. It is but a newspaper squib written at request, but I send you a copy without change.

2. You ask to what extent I question the right of inheritance. The principle already laid down controls the decision respecting inheritance, but the right of inheritance appears to me to be the weakest of all the claims that spring from the theory of personal property. Beyond a sum adequate to the support of those who may be dependent upon a man, I should think a tax upon inheritances perfectly just; the rate of the tax increasing as the blood grows thin. The economic question involved is simply this:—to what extent must we allow men to control their property after death in order to get the best work out of them while they live? And I may add in this connection, that this is also the principle that should decide the

limit of accumulation for men while living; that is to say, which should shape a progressive income tax.

3. You ask to what extent I would advocate state socialism?

I would maintain the post office department under the control of the Federal government, and establish in connection with it a public telegraph and parcel post. I would maintain public education, even to the University, under the control of the States, and establish State forestry and State ownership of mines. I would extend largely the duties of cities, so as to give them control over gas works, water works, and street railways. They should also make the amusements and education of the citizens their care. I trust, on the basis of the above statement, that I shall not be thought ignorant of the inefficiency of local governments at the present time. On the other hand, I would oppose anything like paternal government. Tenement houses at public expense, government insurance for working men, public eating houses and such proposals of mistaken charity, would be injurious to the class whom it is desired to assist; for they would work like the old English poor law.

But it may be that your question rather contemplated the propriety of what is called state interference in industrial action. Two weeks ago I wrote an address upon this subject which was read before the Constitution Club of New York, and is being read this evening before the Institute of Social Science in the same city. It will shortly be in print. In that paper I endeavored to show first, that the dogma of laissez-faire and the principle of free competition are distinct things. The principle was laid down for the guidance of the state, that it should secure society in the enjoyment of the benefits of competitive action, while securing society against its evil workings. I stated both the evils and the benefits of competition, and endeavored from the analysis to discover rules for the guidance of the state.

But without wearying you with such detail, in answer to the question if I am a socialist, I say no. To quote from my lecture on the subject delivered at the University, "The system breaks down when closely scrutinized. It embraces one industrial blunder, one practical impossibility, and one political absurdity." This is the only instance of dogmatism that I indulge in the entire course. It is my wish that our civilization may be saved from the sterility of what is commonly called socialism, and to that end I advocate a further development of proprietary rights and a further development of the science of government.

There is but one word which I wish to add. I confess that I am surprised at the presentation of these questions. My position in the University is such that it would be possible for you to drop me without any action whatever. It does not seem to me that this would be fair. If I go, I want it known why I go. Am I not right in making such a request? For the rest, I feel thankful to you that you have made it unnecessary for me to say anything of my personal wishes in this matter.

This reply has been written hastily and in the press of other work, but I think it represents those views that have grown to be a part of myself.

Very sincerely yours,—

Henry C. Adams

Ann Arbor, Mich., Nov. 18, 1886.

Dear Mr. Lloyd,

I remember you were kind enough to request of me the address I read before the Presbyterian Club in Chicago. A friend of mine in Detroit wanted to read it and kept it some time, and I expected to read it on Monday evening last before a club here. This I state in explanation of delay. But I wrote another on Henry George at the last minute so might have sent this before. I would only say, it is not a finished address by any means. I never take the trouble of correcting anything unless it goes to press.

We were talking of the Anarchists and their trial. I cannot see but it is good law upon which they were convicted; whether the evidence supported the theory or not, I cannot say. And I think you probably are right in saying that no governor would pardon them. The approbation shown in Wisconsin of the action of Gov. Rusk would be too strong as a political consideration against it. And when I keep my judgment on top of my sympathies, I must admit them to be worthy such punishment if ever men are worthy such punishment. But as a matter of expediency it is not all clear.

Men *will not* interpret facts properly, and it seems the claims of the masters have been more unrelenting since the conviction of Anarchists than before. It was shown in your Chicago strikes last week. What we need is a clear cut issue for the working men to fight for; not a dreamy idea. Such an issue I try to suggest in my paper. I should like to know what you think of it. My Detroit friend said the suggestion was impracticable, unjust, and showed want of sound judgment. I am sorry it is not worked out more clearly.

Please remember me to Mrs. Lloyd. I hope to be in a position sometime soon to accept her kind invitation.

Very Sincerely Yours,

Henry C. Adams

Winnetka, Ill., Dec. 6, 1886.

Dear Prof. Adams,

I have been thinking over your paper a great deal, not only because I was interested in it as shadowing forth your future views and conduct, but, because its analysis of the question was so fundamental. I want to write you about it freely, because that is the only kind of compliment that I would venture to make to you, and because the whole matter is so serious that honest people who can discuss it without the help of dynamite had best say to each other just what they think.

Of course you do not expect me to agree with you. Much the greatest part of the excitement got out of the study of Economics comes from the certainty that no matter what doctrine you lay down, nearly every one else in the science will take it up as a wager of battle. But I do not so much disagree with what you say as with what you do not say. Your main points if I have read aright are that we must enforce the responsibility that goes with industrial power, as that belonging to political power has been enforced, and that the "wrongs" in question arise not from the too great individualization of property, but from its too limited individualization or particularization, and finally that the workingmen must work their reforms out between themselves and their employers, without invoking the help of the state, which must be left to settle its own differences with the capitalist class.

Now I am so firmly persuaded that the alternative before us is one of Reform or Revolution; that is, we must either get redress for these "wrongs" through the state or through anarchy that I beg your indulgence for a brief statement of the reasons which make me feel that the line of thought and action you suggest will lead you afield.

What we have before us, already in active operation, is a state of *private war* between two great classes of people. Passions are rising. Conflicts are more frequent. Both sides are irreconcilable. Either side, if successful in its conquest of the other would be anti-social,—despotic, which is anarchist for everything but itself. Neither side represents "the people,"—altho both claim to be their saviors—. The interests of the Commonwealth are unrepresented. The corporations in Pennsylvania like the workingmen in New York grasp at political power only for class purposes. Just as the private wars of the barons of the Middle Ages had to be suppressed by the crown so must this private war of capital and labor be suppressed by the state, i.e., by political action, that is by the organization for certain clearly defined purposes, of those men, who standing for neither combatant, stand for all the people, including the Kilkenny cats themselves, who else will disappear utterly in a cloud of fur and claws.

It is true that private property is not enough particularized with us, whence our fears. But is it not the point of the whole matter, that we have reached this result under our system of saying; Let these interests settle their differences among themselves, and that under this theory, private property has failed to be particularized fairly? The system of "each one for himself," and "no wrong without a remedy" has broken down. Those who think the courts of justice will enforce the responsibility of power forget that the court is an arena where as elsewhere the victory is to the strong and cunning. Who can hope, seeing the attitude of the German aristocracy (alias the government) towards the socialists or workingmen, seeing the similar attitude of the English landlords towards the peasantry, and the Pinkerton mob pointing Winchester rifles out of Chicago

Packing-House windows at the rifleless mob outside, who can hope that these antagonists can settle their quarrels by talk between themselves or by the help of the existing laws? An umpire must appear, a sovereign umpire. That umpire must be begotten out of the people of all classes, it must wield the power of the irresistible State, widened and strengthened to meet this crisis. Just so, the State was new made conturies ago to take out of the hands of classes privileges and power, concerning money, courts, laws, taxes, roads, which in the hands of the few were mischievous beyond endurance; but when taken up by the State became the chief fruits of civilization. The "progress" of the world has placed in the hands of classes powers over the movement of population, over the residence of the people, over their food, amusements, the distribution of the land, the control of machinery, mines, hours, places, conditions of work, which they are using to their advantage to the common disadvantage. We can not leave it to class conferences to enforce the responsibilities of this power; they can be enforced by a power only, stronger than both of them. There is but one such power—the State. The question whether we are to have reform or not is simply a question whether the people upon discussion prove to be intelligent and good enough to be able to cooperate to take upon themselves through the State, for the common good, the powers now misused by a few. Under modern conditions, these "*powers*" over wages, choice of occupation, manner of life, etc., etc., must exist. The question is shall they be controlled, regulated, by the individual or the State. Shall the Rhine belong to the Barons or the people? If the people can assume the umpireship in the struggle, well; if not, not well. But before this great change in our political objects and methods can be made, the very *roots* of our notions about government, and about industrial relations, must be torn up. For the current economics, and politics afford no principles or phrases for use in this crisis. Whether these principles are to emerge from a friendly debate, or from harsher encounters, is the great question of the future—no, the present. You know as well as—better than—I, what history tells us to expect.

Very truly yours,

H. D. Lloyd